The Source for Early Literacy Development

Linda K. Crowe

Sara S. Reichmuth

Skill: Literacy
Ages: Birth through 8 years

LinguiSystems, Inc.
3100 4th Avenue
East Moline, IL 61244-9700

800-776-4332

FAX: 800-577-4555
E-mail: service@linguisystems.com
Web: linguisystems.com

Printed in the U.S.A.

ISBN 10: 0-7606-0331-6
ISBN 13: 978-0-7606-0331-4

About the Authors

Linda K. Crowe, **Ph.D.**, **CCC-SLP**, is an Assistant Professor of Communication Sciences and Disorders in the School of Family Studies and Human Services at Kansas State University. She has been involved in the education of young children for 25 years as a Head Start assistant teacher, an elementary classroom teacher, a school-based speech-language pathologist, and a university instructor. Her experiences also include state and national presentations, school and parent workshops, and child language and literacy research. Linda was instrumental in the development and implementation of an early intervention program involving a partnering of a university, public school, and Head Start agency in Nebraska. She also organized and supervised a parent training program in Louisiana. She has developed procedures for facilitating children's language and literacy development during adult-child storybook reading. These procedures have been reported at state and national conventions and have been published in professional journals.

Sara S. Reichmuth, **Ph.D.**, **CCC-SLP**, is an Assistant Professor of Communication Disorders in the Communication Disorders Program at Arkansas State University. She has been involved in literacy development for children and adults for 15 years as a school-based speech-language pathologist, consultant, and university instructor. Sara served as the Consultant and Service Provider for a Family Literacy Training Grant in Louisiana, working with adults with limited literacy skills. She was involved in a workshop to train teachers in reading intervention for incarcerated juveniles. Sara's experiences also include state and national presentations, and research in the development of phonological awareness in kindergarten children and reading intervention for children and adults.

The Source for Early Literacy Development is Linda and Sara's first publication with LinguiSystems.

Illustrations by Margaret Warner

Cover design by Mike Paustian

Table of Contents

Carmen grabs a book within her reach and happily begins to chew. Upon seeing her interest in the book, Carmen's mother comments, "Oh, you want to read your book."

Mom picks Carmen up and places her on her lap. As Mom takes the book from Carmen's mouth, she turns the book right-side up and begins to point to and name objects pictured in the book.

This event and other literacy experiences are repeated throughout Carmen's formative years. Carmen's mother, like many other parents, is laying the foundation for later literacy success.

Although literacy is typically viewed as conventional reading and writing, the process of learning to read begins at birth. The early behaviors associated with literacy development have become known as **emergent literacy**. Sulzby (1989) defines emergent literacy as "the reading and writing behaviors of young children that precede and develop into conventional literacy" (p. 88). This period of emergent literacy typically encompasses birth through age eight and is characterized by children's growth in oral and written language development. This amazing growth in language does not just happen, but rather it is supported and facilitated through the interactions of more competent language users in the child's environment.

The Oral and Written Language Connection

Language is a socially-shared code used to communicate (Halliday, 1978). Young children learn oral language first. They learn new words and come to master the basics of English word order long before entering school. Although written language shares the same underlying processes as oral language in terms of vocabulary, grammar, word endings, and so forth, written language is represented in a more abstract form than oral language.

In spoken language, the physical context serves to support the speaker's message. A word can be communicated by pointing to or looking at an object. A message can be clarified when the speaker sees that the listener has not understood or when the listener asks for more information. The face-to-face nature of oral language allows the speaker to be less concise and explicit in the words used without losing meaning. Grammatically-incomplete utterances are acceptable as both the speaker and the listener mentally fill in implied information. Oral language also allows the speaker to enhance the message or develop nuances of meaning by using loudness, pitch, rate, and other vocal patterns.

To express or understand written messages requires using words to represent the physical environment that is no longer shared between the reader and the writer. The words used to communicate the message must be explicit enough to create the physical environment and the characters' thoughts, feelings, and states of mind. The written words must be clear and explicit because the reader and writer are not in the same physical setting. Further, to enhance a message, written language requires a different set of conventions to represent the vocal patterns present in oral language.

Although written language is an extension of spoken language, it is more than oral language written down. It requires the knowledge and understanding of another set of symbols. Speech consists of sounds and writing consists of letters. Because written language is a visual symbol system, it is a more abstract representation of speech. In addition, the sounds of oral language do not map directly onto the orthographic system of written language. Becoming competent in understanding and using the symbols of written language typically is a process that requires more time to develop than oral language, although both are learned in a similar manner in similar contexts.

Social-Constructivist Theory

According to social-constructivist theory, language develops in a social context (Vygotsky, 1978). Within this context, children experience language being used for meaningful and purposeful reasons. Children actively participate in the communicative events and are supported in their learning by more competent language users.

Parents and other adults use strategies to help their children communicate and learn language. Bruner (1967) refers to this assistance as a **scaffold**. Scaffolds include visual and verbal prompts to engage children in purposeful interactions. As children display competence in a given skill, adults gradually withdraw the scaffolds; in other words, adults reduce the amount and type of support they provide. Carmen's mother provided a natural scaffold by orienting the book in the right direction and turning the pages from front to back. Once Carmen demonstrated proper book orientation on her own, the orienting scaffold was no longer needed. As Carmen acquires and demonstrates other new skills, her mother will adjust the amount of assistance provided.

Carmen's mother intuitively knew that her assistance was most effective when it occurred within Carmen's **Zone of Proximal Development (ZPD)** (Vygotsky, 1978). According to Vygotsky, the ZPD represents a continuum of learning. The lower limit of learning is defined as "the child's level of independent performance." The upper limit represents the point at which the child is unable to perform even with assistance. The developmental zone between these two boundaries represents a child's performance when given assistance. Optimal learning occurs within this zone. In Carmen's case, the lower limit of the ZPD was represented by her chewing on the book (independent performance). With the assistance of her mother, Carmen oriented the book for reading (mediated performance) but did not have the language competence to point to or label pictures (performance limit).

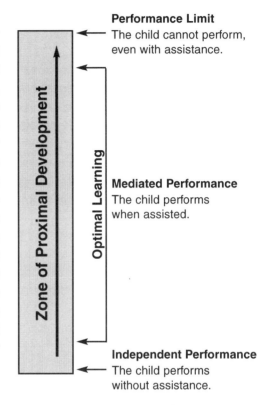

Performance Limit
The child cannot perform, even with assistance.

Mediated Performance
The child performs when assisted.

Independent Performance
The child performs without assistance.

Children are immersed in language-promoting environments. When immersed in these real communicative events, children are facilitated to participate as fully contributing members. They use the sounds and patterns of the adult language. They use single words and word combinations to express an expanding knowledge of their world. They engage in purposeful interactions to communicate their wants and needs. As children continue to listen to and engage in meaningful interactions, they develop more complex ways of communicating. Within a short time, children are well on their way to mastering the social, linguistic, and cultural rules of their world.

At the same time children are immersed in oral language, they are surrounded by written language. Parents write down phone messages and pay bills. They read recipes and read with their children. They dress their children in clothes that have printed messages and buy toys imprinted with letters and pictures. They supply the tools of literacy, such as crayons, pencils, markers, coloring books, and paper. Adults provide these early experiences with the expectation that children will become literate.

The Purpose and Overview of This Book

The Source for Early Literacy Development is a resource on children's emergent reading and writing from birth through age eight. This work brings together the research from respected and well-known authorities on emergent literacy. The purpose of this book is twofold.

- One purpose is to provide professionals with **background information** on reading and writing development in preschool children. Literacy is typically viewed as reading printed words or writing letters and words. Literacy behaviors, however, are demonstrated long before conventional reading and writing occur. It is critical for professionals to recognize behaviors that signal the child's current state of literacy development. Once these behaviors are identified, the facilitator can move the child along the developmental continuum.

- A second purpose is to provide professionals with **strategies** to facilitate literacy development. The strategies described are appropriate for any young child. Most importantly, these strategies allow for natural, communicative interactions that promote children's meaningful and successful literacy learning. It is our hope that, through the work of skilled professionals, all children will attain the literacy skills necessary for academic success and discover how reading and writing can enrich their lives.

This book is divided into three parts:

Part I: Understanding Reading

Part II: Understanding Writing

Part III: Activities and Sources

Part I begins with a description of the typical progression of reading development, followed by characteristics and factors that may promote or inhibit reading acquisition. Subsequent chapters describe strategies used to facilitate early reading. Transcripts demonstrating the use of facilitation strategies also are included. Part I concludes with sample reading goals and objectives.

Writing development is outlined in **Part II**. A general progression of writing development is described. Facilitation strategies for promoting writing are discussed, and specific examples of use are provided. Part II concludes with sample writing goals and objectives.

Part III includes reading and writing activities for preschool children. Suggestions for working with parents and families are provided. Finally, lists of children's books and professional references are included.

Children progress at different rates in their reading development. This development is influenced by the frequency and types of reading experiences children encounter early in their lives. Young children who are read to on a regular basis have been found to exhibit a similar progression of reading behaviors. The following information discusses the typical ages at which these early reading behaviors occur. Use these stages as a guide for identifying a child's current level of reading performance, not as an indicator of delay in reading development.

Developmental Progression

Object-Focused Preverbal Children (0-18 months)

During the first year-and-a-half of life, an infant explores books in perceptual ways and in a manner similar to manipulation of other objects in the infant's world. Early experiences with books highlight the child's sensorimotor exploration of unfamiliar objects.

The child pays little attention to books at first, attending only when the book directly impacts his or her body. When the adult brings the book to the child, the child explores the book through sensorimotor behaviors by touching, mouthing, or dropping it (Monroe, 1969).

By eight months of age, children display emerging intentional behaviors (Westby, 1991). With increases in purposeful behavior, young children also become more discriminate in their explorations. They begin to reach out to and focus attention to books. While being read to, children touch the book, begin to flip randomly through the pages, and show interest in some of the pictures. This attention to the pictures is encouraged by adults who point to or tap on the pictures to draw the children's attention to something of interest.

Between 12 and 18 months of age, children increase their interest in the pictures. Children continue to enjoy manipulating a book, but also observe the behaviors and language of adults as they read a story, learning new functions for the book.

Picture-Focused Beginning Talkers (12-36 months)

Children during this period of reading development exhibit intentional behaviors directed toward the pictures in the book. Children show increasing interest in the pictures and express pre-narrative verbalizations about the story. Children come to realize that the pictures represent real events in the world during this stage of reading development.

Children enjoy the social contact and turn-taking that occurs during reading. They locate favorite storybooks and sit on the adult's lap to have the story read. As the adult reads, the child pats or touches the pictured objects and points to the pictures to direct the adult's attention to something of interest. These gestures are often accompanied by environmental noises, such as motor or animal sounds; proto-words, such as *ba-ba* and *ki-ki*; and, eventually, words to label people and actions, such as *mommy* and *night-night.*

Children also develop book orientation abilities during this period of reading growth. They recognize when the book is right-side-up versus upside-down and turn the pages from the front to the back of the book.

As children gain experience with books and advance in linguistic and cognitive abilities, they name familiar objects either spontaneously or when asked simple *who, what,* or *where* questions. They show increased interest in learning new or unfamiliar information and ask simple questions about the pictures.

> Child: (points to a picture) That?
>   What's that?

At the end of this period of reading development, children understand that the pictured information represents ongoing activities or events. They may talk about a character's actions and ask for favorite stories to be read and reread. Children participate in the rereading of familiar stories by providing a repeating phrase, story line, or rhyming part. These beginning talkers label and comment, but no story can be inferred from their remarks. These children are contextually bound to the pictures, and their utterances are uninterpretable without the pictures present.

> Child: Look, a mouse.
>
>   There he goes.
>
>   Huff and puff.

Picture-Focused Conversationalists (3-5 years)

During this stage of reading development, children demonstrate advances in knowledge about stories by describing the actions and events that occur. This period shows a progression of oral narrative development from collections of information around a central theme to retelling major story events and sequences (Applebee, 1978; Norris & Hoffman, 1993).

1. Children recognize that the pictures represent actions and events that occur in the real world. Children will talk to the characters.

   Child: Don't worry, little bear.

2. Children react to characters' actions with emotional responses.

   Child: He thinks that's yucky.

3. Children remember larger portions of stories, especially for favorite books that are read frequently. Children will use an oral narrative style to retell main story events.

   Child: He tried to water the plants, but he spilled all the water.

4. Children also anticipate and predict events that will occur on future pages of the story. This level is characterized by pretending to read parts of the story.

   Child: (holds the book as if reading) Next he goes to bed.

Picture-Focused Oral-Literate Transition (4-5 years)

As children gain more experience with books and begin to use language that can refer to events and happenings removed in time and space, they also show greater understanding of stories and learn new ways to talk about stories. During this stage, children move from oral language-like stories to more literate, language-like narratives (Sulzby, 1985). Their "reading" of favorite or familiar stories contains elements of written language found in books.

   Child: Once upon a time, there was a little boy who blew bubbles.

Children demonstrate understanding that print communicates the stories represented in the pictures, as shown by statements such as *Read the words* and by questions such as *What does it say?* Children also know when portions of familiar stories are skipped or paraphrased.

   Child: You didn't read this part.

Children provide evidence of print awareness. They recognize, point to, and name familiar letters or identify letters in familiar words.

Child: That's a *T*.

   This says my name right here.

Children's emergent reading becomes more conventional as they point to the print while relating a written, language-like story. This behavior includes reciting memorized portions of the story verbatim, with the retelling matching the printed words on the page. Nearing the end of this stage, children begin to recognize individual words and point word-by-word to the text as they retell a memorized portion of text.

Print-Focused Beginning Readers (4-8 years)

As children develop more concepts about print and understand that the function of print is to communicate the story, they often refuse to read when asked to read or tell parts of the story. For example, children will say, "I can't read" or "I don't know the words." Their fluid oral narratives may become slow, labored attempts to sound out words or to read familiar sight words. This period of refusal is typically short-lived, but it is a common phenomenon observed during reading development. This behavior subsides once children acquire more strategies for making the print meaningful.

Children's transition into conventional reading also may be accompanied by poor story comprehension. As they attempt to read the words independently, the focus on decoding the words may result in the children losing the meaning of what the print conveys.

From ages five to eight, children acquire more sight vocabulary and understanding of the alphabetic principle (sound-symbol associations). They read more fluently, but they often use one reading strategy to the exclusion of others, such as grapho-phonemic (focus on sound-symbol association) or syntactic (focus on the sentence structure). Children's comprehension improves during this period of time, but their reading is not yet proficient.

Reading competence is demonstrated as children use multiple strategies to read text, including the integration of grapho-phonemic, semantic (what makes sense in the context and use of picture clues), and syntactic components of print. This conventional reading generally is realized by a child's eighth birthday; however, there is considerable variability across children.

Early Reading Checklist

The Early Reading Checklist (pages 15-16) provides a guide for professionals to use in observing a young child's reading behaviors. The checklist is arranged in a hierarchy of reading development from the earliest unintentional behaviors to the emergence of conventional reading. The Early Reading Checklist includes some of the distinguishing behaviors children exhibit at different stages of early reading development.

There are a number of ways in which the professional may observe a child's reading behaviors. The following procedures are provided only as a general guide to assist the professional in completing the observations:

- Live observations are possible, but a video recording of the readings will allow for a more thorough appraisal of behaviors. If possible, more than one reading opportunity should occur, with observations taking place on two or three different days.

- Observations can be completed during a group reading time, during a parent-child reading time in the home, or during any adult-child shared reading time. You may want to observe the child's reading behaviors across different settings to obtain a more comprehensive profile. It is also desirable to make the observations during spontaneous or naturally-occurring reading opportunities.

Here are some general considerations for using the Early Reading Checklist:

- Select a book appropriate to the child's perceived level of development. (A list of potential books is provided on the following page.) The observer or reading participant should simply hand the book to a preverbal child. For a child beyond the preverbal level, position the book upside down and backwards. You may also use a verbal prompt, such as "Read me this story."

- Develop simple reading prompts using the facilitation strategies outlined in Chapter 3, pages 30-61, keeping in mind that the reading interactions should be natural communicative exchanges.

- Make periodic observations to note changes in a child's reading over time.

Suggested Books

Preverbal

Ahlberg, J., & Ahlberg, A. (1981). *Peek-A-Boo!* New York: Penguin Books.

Elliott, R. (1996). *My Cuddly Toys.* Kuttawa, KY: McClanahan Book Company.

Quinlan, P. M. (1996). *Baby's Feet.* North York, Ontario, Canada: Annick Press.

Beginning Talkers

Aruego, J., & Dewey, A. (1989). *Five Little Ducks.* New York: Crown Publishers.

Carle, E. (1996). *Brown Bear, Brown Bear, What Do You See?* New York: Henry Holt.

Mayer, M. (1983). *Little Critter's This Is My House.* Racine, WI: Western Publishing.

Conversational Through Beginning Readers

Christelow, E. (1989). *Five Little Monkeys.* New York: Clarion Books.

Galdone, P. (1973). *The Little Red Hen.* New York: Scholastic.

Galdone, P. (1970). *The Three Little Pigs.* New York: Clarion Books.

Galdone, P. (1973). *The Three Bears.* New York: Scholastic.

Mayer, M. (1975). *Just for You.* Racine, WI: Western Publishing.

Mayer, M. (1983). *When I Get Bigger.* Racine, WI: Western Publishing.

Zeifert, H. (1995). *The Three Billy Goats Gruff.* New York: Tambourine Books.

Early Reading Checklist

Child's name _____ Age _____

Book title _____ Setting _____

Observer _____ Date _____

Check all listed or similar behaviors observed. Note similar behaviors beside those listed. Comment at the end of this checklist on other factors observed, such as fussing, inattention, participant behaviors, environmental factors, etc.

Object-Focused Preverbal Child (0-18 months)

_____ mouths, bangs, chews, or drops book

_____ needs book brought close to touch or to look at pictures

_____ reaches out to book

_____ flips pages randomly

_____ looks at pictures momentarily

_____ begins to imitate adult (e.g., says "vroom" or "meow")

Picture-Focused Beginning Talker (12-36 months)

_____ listens as adult reads

_____ pats and points to pictures

_____ makes noises in response to pictures (e.g., motor or animal sounds)

_____ names some pictures

_____ demonstrates book orientation

_____ performs some actions represented in pictures

_____ names familiar people or objects

_____ turns pages back and forth at random

_____ asks simple questions (e.g., "What that?" or "Who that?")

_____ talks about own actions (e.g., "Brush teeth" or "Drink juice.")

_____ participates in reciting repetitive story lines or rhyming parts

_____ tells portions of stories (e.g., "He's washing.")

Picture-Focused Conversationalist (3-5 years)

_____ talks to characters

_____ reacts to characters' actions (e.g., "The frog's jumping.")

_____ reacts to characters' emotions (e.g., makes sad face and says, "He's sad.")

_____ begins to pretend read using language that sounds like oral stories

_____ retells some story events in an oral language style

_____ anticipates and predicts parts of stories

Picture-Focused Oral-to-Literate Transition (4-5 years)

_____ knows that print tells you what to say

_____ recognizes letters (points to and names familiar letters)

_____ knows when portions of stories are skipped

_____ pretends to read using language that sounds like written stories

_____ repeats favorite parts of stories verbatim

_____ tracks whole lines of text with finger while repeating parts of stories

_____ points to individual words while pretending to read

Print-Focused Beginning Reader (4-8 years)

_____ refuses to read unfamiliar words or stories

_____ reads portions of text by sounding out words or reading sight words

_____ fails to comprehend unfamiliar stories read independently

_____ reads using multiple strategies (e.g., sounding out, predicting, and using pictures)

_____ reads story fluently with appropriate rate and phrasing

Comments

_____

_____

_____

_____

_____

_____

_____

_____

_____

_____

Note: Based on Monroe (1969), Norris (1992; 1999b), & Sulzby (1985).

Six-year-old Mia and her mother sit down to read one of Mia's favorite books. Mia's mother reads the title, then quickly turns to the first page and starts reading. Her reading rate is quite rapid, and she does not pause to talk about the pictures, ask Mia questions, or comment on the story. As Mia's mother finishes reading the words on each page, she says, "Page." Given this cue, Mia turns the page, then sits, listens a little, and looks around the room. In less than two minutes, the book is finished and put away.

This scenario seems far from the typical parent-child reading so frequently described in books and reports, yet these reading behaviors are not uncommon between parents and their children who have language and learning problems. Mia is a child who has severe articulation problems and is also exhibiting difficulty in learning to read. Mia's mother is quite concerned, but like many parents of children with disabilities, she does not know how to verbally engage Mia in their joint reading ventures. As a result of Mia's speech and language impairment, a perpetuating cycle has developed in which Mia waits for her cue to turn the page while her mother reads the story.

In the past, Mia's mother tried to enlist Mia's verbal participation by asking questions, but Mia's responses were often unintelligible. To get accurate and identifiable responses to her queries about the story, Mia's mother asked Mia to provide nonverbal behaviors, such as turning the pages of the book. Since Mia was successful in responding to these requests, her mother continued to read with Mia in this manner.

Learning to read is a complex psycholinguistic process and is probably the single, most valued skill of modern society. Most children learn to read as effortlessly as they learn to talk. Increasingly, professionals and researchers are interested in understanding how young children accomplish this feat in a relatively short period of time. This interest is not only to understand typical development, but also to identify those behaviors and other factors that impact children's success or failure in learning to read.

Chapter 1 outlined a general progression of early reading behaviors; however, the rate of that development is highly variable across children. This chapter will discuss behaviors and at-risk factors that impact a child's early reading development.

Reading depends upon many skills, including attention, memory, language, and motivation (Snow, Burns, & Griffin, 1998). Social, cultural, and environmental factors also contribute to a child's experiences and interest in reading. Other factors, such as cognitive ability, hearing status, and speech-language competence, further impact a child's success in learning to read (Snow et al., 1998). These skills and factors interact and differentially influence a child's emergent literacy development.

Snow, Burns, and Griffin (1998) identified the following individual and group factors associated with poor reading achievement:

Individual Factors

- The child has a family history of reading difficulties.

- The child experiences few home literacy experiences.

- The child exhibits early language delay or impairment.

- The child has a hearing impairment.

Group Factors

- The child attends a school in which there is generalized low achievement.

- The child is from a low-income family in an impoverished neighborhood.

- The child has limited English proficiency.

- The child speaks a substantially different dialect of English than is used in school.

These individual and group factors influence a child's understanding and use of oral and written language. The following sections discuss these general indicators as they are manifested in children's specific reading behaviors and with regard to research relevant to these factors.

Behavioral Indicators

The behavioral indicators listed in the box on page 19 and following discussion are not all-inclusive and are not absolute predictors of future reading difficulties. These behaviors often occur during the typical progression of a child's early reading development and should only be considered problematic if they persist into the later preschool years. These behavioral indicators are presented to increase the professional's awareness of early symptoms associated with problems in learning to read. The professional can then monitor the child's progress in literacy development or take preventative measures by providing early reading facilitation.

Behavioral Indicators of Early Literacy Problems

1. Fusses and refuses to look at books or pictures

2. Flips the pages in the book but shows no interest in the story

3. Exhibits poor attention

4. Sits passively as the adult reads (does not question or comment)

5. Responds nonverbally to adult queries

6. Tells oral narratives, but does not use literate language to talk about stories

7. Evidences a general lack of symbol development (playing, drawing, talking)

8. Exhibits poor phonological-awareness abilities

9. Demonstrates early language and/or articulation problems

1. Fussing and Refusing to Look at Books or Pictures

Children who have not progressed to a level in which books are viewed as a social context for communicating often try to avoid book-reading activities. If the adult attempts to read the words or talk about the pictures, the child will try to leave or cry, as in the following example:

> Libby is sitting and playing with a toy. Mother sits down with Libby to read a book. Libby eagerly climbs onto Mother's lap. Then Mother grabs a nearby book. As Mother opens the book, Libby begins to kick, scream, and climb off Mother's lap. Libby happily returns to playing alone with her toy.

2. Flipping Pages Without Attending to the Story

Children may be more interested in the physical properties of a book than in its content. When this happens, children may want to turn the pages but disengage in the activity if the adult tries to read the story or talk about the pictures. Children at this object-focused stage of reading development behave this way because they have not progressed to a more symbolic level of book use, as in the following example:

> Dad and D.J. are sitting side-by-side on the sofa. Dad is reading a book as D.J. looks around the room. D.J. tries to turn the pages, but Dad wants to continue reading. Dad explains, "I'm not finished reading yet." D.J. loses interest and climbs off the sofa.

3. Poor Attention

The ability to attend is essential to language and reading development. A child not only must be able to maintain focus on the pictures, but also must attend to the shapes of letters and letter combinations that make up the words on the page. These letters and words must then be interpreted as meaningful representations of spoken language.

Inattention in young children has been consistently linked to difficulty in language acquisition and poor early literacy development (Lonigan et al., 1999). Preschool children who are unable to maintain attention show difficulty on reading readiness tasks, such as print knowledge and phonological awareness (e.g., rhyming or identifying sounds as being the same or different). The impact of poor attention also has been found to persist into the school years. Approximately 50% of school-aged children with attention deficits experience difficulty in reading (Shaywitz & Shaywitz, 1993).

When a child can neither attend to nor focus on the pictures and print, early reading experiences often result in limited learning or faulty learning about the reading process. It is unclear whether the inattention results in failure to acquire early reading skills or if generalized difficulty in language learning underlies the inattention and emergent reading problems.

4. Sitting Passively As the Adult Reads

Children developing normally often sit and listen to stories as the adult reads (Kaderavek & Sulzby, 1998). In fact, typically-developing children may insist that the adult "just read the words" rather than try to talk about the story. Children with language impairments and/or learning disabilities also may sit passively during adult-child book reading (Crowe in press; Crowe et al., 2000). These children who are at risk for reading problems may sit quietly because they don't understand the story or lack the verbal skills to contribute to and find out more about the story.

5. Participating Nonverbally

Many children actively participate in adult-child book-reading by turning pages and pointing to pictures. These behaviors occur frequently with children at the nonverbal and object-focused stage of reading development. However, preschool children beyond age two who exhibit early language and literacy delay tend to display fewer verbal language behaviors during joint book-reading (Crowe et al., 2000; Marvin & Wright, 1997). Instead, these children often participate nonverbally when adults read books with them.

These nonverbal behaviors include pointing to the pictures, turning the pages of the book, and making environmental sounds, such as animal and motor noises. For children with speech and language delays, these types of participation may be encouraged by adults who do not understand the children's verbal attempts but are able to identify and interpret their children's nonverbal communicative behaviors.

6. Failing to Make the Oral-to-Literate Transition

Typically-developing children as young as two years of age begin to tell oral narratives and produce emergent readings of books (Kaderavek & Sulzby, 1997). Children with early language impairments and/or other learning problems, though, may not develop narrative skills or produce written, language-like stories until they are much older.

Because literate language must be more specific, and in some cases more formal and complex, children at risk for reading difficulty may struggle in learning and using this more advanced language register. Telling an oral, language-like narrative is often supported and supplemented by the pictures. Telling literate narratives requires children to use specific language that can tell the story without the pictures, establishing the time and place of the events and describing the movements and verbalizations of the characters. Children at risk for reading difficulties are often slow to make the transition from the oral to the literate narrative style of storytelling and reading.

7. General Lack of Symbol Development

Learning to read requires a child to understand pictures as representations of ongoing actions and written symbols as representations of oral language describing and elaborating upon the pictured events. The transition to symbol use occurs quite early for typically-developing children. In contrast, children with disabilities or different learning systems may plateau at a pre-symbolic level for many months (or sometimes years) before developing symbol use (Westby, 1991). This slow development may be observed across all areas of children's symbol development, including their play, drawing, and verbal language abilities.

8. Poor Phonological Awareness

One of the most prevalent indicators of reading disability in children is poor phonological awareness. **Phonological awareness** is the ability to talk about the sounds and sound structure of a language (Mattingly, 1972). Reading requires a child to use this knowledge of sound-symbol correspondence to decode printed words. Fluent reading is thought to depend on mastering this explicit knowledge.

Reports consistently indicate that poor readers have difficulty segmenting words into sounds and syllables (Kamhi et al., 1988). For very young children, early indicators of phonological awareness problems may be manifested in an inability to do rhyming, alliteration, and other word manipulations. However, the influences of phonological awareness and reading are probably bidirectional; good readers have good phonological awareness abilities and vice versa (Snyder & Downey, 1997).

Tasks of phonological awareness include these:

Word Segmentation	Tap the number of syllables in the word *baseball*.
Rhyming	What rhymes with *cat*?
Alliteration	What's another word that begins like *soap*?
Word Manipulation	Change the /t/ in *cat* to /n/.

9. Early Language and/or Articulation Problems

Because oral language skills provide the foundation for written language development, children who exhibit difficulty in acquiring and understanding spoken language are significantly at risk for later reading problems (Aram & Hall, 1989). Measures of children's early language development have been used to predict which children will experience later reading and academic challenges. Language measures have included knowledge and production of general vocabulary, sentence structure (length and complexity), discourse functions, and phonological ability.

Although certain components of language competency have been associated with reading problems, overall language ability is probably the best predictor of reading success or failure. Specific areas of language found to correlate with later poor reading include the following (see Snyder & Downey [1997] for a review):

- poor speed and accuracy in naming pictures and objects

- delays in syntactic knowledge assessed through cloze procedure

- inability to retell stories in a complete narrative structure

- delayed oral speech development

- inability to manipulate speech sounds

Children with speech and language impairments often disengage or refuse to engage in shared book activities and produce few or limited utterances during reading (Kaderavek & Sulzby, 1998; Marvin & Mirenda, 1993). These children seldom choose books to share with adults and often persist in sensorimotor exploration of books beyond the expected age. Children with specific language impairments are slow in their development of emergent reading skills (Kaderavek & Sulzby, 1998). More common reading behaviors of children with language delays include nonverbal interactions with books, labeling and describing pictures, and commenting on the actions of the characters or objects in stories (Crowe, in press).

Social, Cultural, and Environmental Factors

"Children who are particularly likely to have difficulty learning to read in the primary grades are those who begin school with less prior knowledge and skill in certain domains, most notably letter knowledge, phonological sensitivity, familiarity with the basic purposes and mechanisms of reading, and language ability." (Snow et al., 1998, p. 137).

The following social, cultural, and environmental factors are associated with children's early literacy development:

Social, Cultural, and Environmental Factors

1. Home literacy experiences

2. Socioeconomic status

3. Cultural differences

4. Dialectal and first-language differences

1. Home Literacy Experiences

Home literacy experiences and the value placed on learning to read and write significantly impact a child's interest in and later success with learning to read. Listed in the box below are five factors Kaderavek and Sulzby (2000) believe are associated with learning to read.

Positive Literacy Experiences

1. **Children become socialized to literacy.**

   Children learn the social discourse of reading by engaging in real literacy activities; a literacy-enriched environment promotes literacy development.

2. **Children develop complex language abilities through adult-child reading.**

   Frequent reading experiences facilitate children's acquisition of new vocabulary words; varied discourse functions; longer, more complex sentences; and de-contextualized language associated with a literate language style. These adult-child reading experiences acquaint the child with the written language register, promote competency in emergent literacy, and facilitate long-term achievement in reading.

3. **Children experience positive changes in literate language through repeated reading of books.**

   Reading the same book repeatedly with young children is associated with changes in their ability to talk about a story. Children's language progresses from picture-focused discussions to print-focused talk, such as word meanings, familiar letters, etc.

4. **Children are provided more complex language models.**

   Adult talk about the story and the printed text often is different from what children hear on a daily basis. The written language found in stories often is more formal and explicit than conversational language.

5. **Children from different ethnic and socioeconomic backgrounds differ in their literacy experiences.**

   Most families frequently read with young children, but not all social and cultural groups engage in the same types of language and literacy activities with their children.

The social, cultural, and environmental factors listed in the box on page 23 have been associated with young children's learning to read. Despite considerable variability across cultures, children with typical language and learning systems often are successful in learning to read. In contrast, the social, cultural, and environmental elements listed in the box below place children at risk for reading difficulties (Hess & Holloway, 1984).

Risk Factors

• Extent to which literacy is valued

Children experience fewer reading problems in families that view reading as important. These families model reading and engage children frequently in reading experiences.

• Expectations for reading achievement

Children learn to read when they are read with and when their attempts to read receive positive responses from others.

• Provision of literacy materials

Children need exposure to a variety of literacy materials, including books, magazines, and writing supplies.

• Frequency and type of adult-child reading experiences

Children who have frequent reading experiences listen attentively to stories being read. These children also develop literate language knowledge when adults respond to their questions and comments about the pictures and stories.

• Frequency of verbal interactions

Children who have frequent verbal interactions with adults also demonstrate competency in vocabulary knowledge and general language ability (Hart & Risley, 1999). This verbal interaction includes not only reading books with children but also engaging children in conversation throughout the day.

Children who have few early experiences reading books are at a disadvantage when they enter school and begin more formal reading instruction. Limited book experiences frequently translate to little understanding about printed text. Increasingly, educators expect children to begin kindergarten with knowledge of letters, words, and print. Although many children catch up once formal reading instruction begins, there may be resultant social and emotional stigma associated with remedial instruction.

Children who are poor readers often have generalized deficits in language abilities. These children's linguistic differences may then limit their social interactional opportunities and cause them to withdraw or be rejected by peers (Brinton & Fujiki, 1993; Gertner et al., 1994). The effects of social withdrawal and peer rejection often continue throughout these children's academic careers and into adulthood.

2. Socioeconomic Status

Socioeconomic status (SES) is generally determined on the basis of family income, educational achievement, or occupation. As a group, families from low-income areas often are less educated and frequently live in environments with poor health conditions.

Children from lower-income families are at higher risk for difficulty in learning to read (Juel et al., 1986; Smith & Dixon, 1995). Significant differences have been found between middle-SES and low-SES children in emergent literacy abilities, including oral language, phonological sensitivity, lexical access, and print knowledge. These differences are attributed, in part, to the availability of books to be read and the language- and literacy-promoting practices in the homes of poor children (Chall & Curtis, 1991). Meeting children's daily needs often takes precedence over adult-child reading and other literacy activities.

The impact of SES on a child's reading development is less obvious at ages five or six but more noticeable when reading becomes more complex (Chall & Curtis, 1991). Reading school texts and other literary genre, such as poetry, novels, and plays, requires knowledge of less-familiar words and language patterns that may not occur in many low-SES neighborhoods. Additionally, living in a low-SES community and attending a school in an impoverished neighborhood is more detrimental to a child's language and literacy competence than for a child living in a low-SES home and attending a middle-SES school (Snow et al., 1998). The relationship between reading achievement and SES shows a large gap between the achievement of disadvantaged urban children and advantaged age peers. The longer poor children remain in school, the wider the reading achievement gap becomes.

3. Cultural Differences

A number of cultural differences exist in parent-child interaction patterns and adult-child storybook reading practices. In some cultures, a child's active verbal participation is neither encouraged nor desired. Instead, children are taught language and communicative functions by observing adults engage in verbal exchanges (Damico & Damico, 1993; Kay-Raining Bird & Vetter, 1994; Ochs, 1986).

Reading practices also are quite variable across cultures. The typical adult-child focusing behavior of directing a child's attention toward objects (i.e., storybooks) is not universal (Heath, 1983). In some Japanese cultures (Bornstein et al., 1990) and many African-American homes (Heath, 1983), mothers prefer face-to-face communicative exchanges over object-focused discussions with their children.

Active verbal participation in the form of questions and comments about books are common occurrences during typical reading routines, yet there is evidence to suggest that a mother's questions and questioning behaviors may be culture specific. Anderson-Yockel and Haynes (1994) observed that during mother-child storybook reading, African-American mothers asked fewer *yes/no* questions and *wh-* questions than European-American mothers. Similarly, Hispanic mothers ask their children few questions about obvious, known information, such as asking their children to label or describe pictures in a book (Langdon & Cheng, 1992).

4. Dialectal and First-Language Differences

When a preschool child's home language is not primarily English, the ease of learning to read printed English is likely to be impeded to some extent, particularly if reading instruction in English begins before the child has acquired oral proficiency in English. (Snow et al., 1998, p. 123)

A child who speaks an English dialect that differs significantly from the printed English found in books also may experience difficulty in learning to read. Dialectal differences and English as a second language do not in and of themselves pose significant problems in learning to read. Other factors often limit early reading experiences for these children. Many children with dialectal and first-language differences also come from high-risk communities. That is, children who live in impoverished neighborhoods, grow up in cultures that differ dramatically from the school environment, and are perceived negatively by educators due to their language difference are more at risk for reading problems than other children (Snow et al., 1998). It is, therefore, quite difficult to determine the extent to which dialectal and language differences alone impact a child's learning to read.

Despite known cultural differences in adult-child social routines, literacy experiences, and linguistic environments, expectations for children at school entry remain fairly consistent across the nation. Therefore, early language and literacy experiences remain a critical factor in a child's later reading success.

Summary

Children who do not learn to read or who learn to read only marginally are disadvantaged throughout their lives, socially and occupationally. Difficulty in learning to read may occur for a variety of reasons and, most likely, is attributable to a combination of factors. Since many children do not learn to read conventionally before entering school, parents and primary caregivers may be unaware of behaviors that indicate potential problems in learning to read.

Although cognitive deficits, hearing impairments, and a family history of reading problems are known contributors to future reading difficulties, these factors have not been directly addressed in this chapter. Instead, this chapter has focused on and described behavioral indicators and social, cultural, and environmental factors found to impact a child's early reading development. There are no clearly-defined guidelines to determine early reading problems, and early detection of reading difficulty is often speculative.

The lists in the box on page 29 provide a summary of factors found to contribute to a child's reading success or failure. These factors are only general findings and are not considered all-inclusive. The findings are important for early detection and intervention to alleviate the impact that these factors have on oral and written language development. For children who exhibit early delays or who come from high-risk environments, reading facilitation should begin early and should be monitored for effectiveness.

Factors Influencing Reading Development

Within-Child Factors

Known cognitive deficits

Generalized delays in all areas of development

Hearing impairment

Speech-language impairment

Delay in oral narrative development

Poor attention

Difficulty with phonological-awareness tasks

Family history of reading problems

Difficulty learning concepts of print (letters, words, where to read, etc.)

Social-Environmental Factors

Low socioeconomic environment

English as a second language

Dialectal difference

Different literacy experiences from school expectations

Limited language and literacy experiences

Importance of Early Reading Experiences

Reading aloud with children is probably the single, most important activity for facilitating children's emergent reading behaviors (Wells, 1985). Quality reading experiences occur when books are carefully selected and used in developmentally appropriate ways that encourage active child participation (Whitehurst et al., 1994). The central goal of early reading experiences is to enhance children's exposure to print and to facilitate children's ability to communicate and symbolize using print (Clay, 1979; Teale & Sulzby, 1986).

Learning to communicate through books and print requires an integration of multiple processes, including linguistic, social, cognitive, and sensorimotor (Sulzby 1985). This integration can be facilitated or inhibited by the choice of books, the language used to talk about the books, and the manner in which books are used with children. High-quality adult-child storybook reading occurs when the adult facilitator presents the story at a level that is appropriate to the developmental needs of the child, or within the child's **Zone of Proximal Development (ZPD)** (Vygotsky, 1978; see page 7).

Whereas all children benefit from book-reading experiences that are appropriate to their developmental needs, it is even more critical for the adult facilitator to modify reading interactions with children who are progressing slowly in their development of emergent literacy skills (Klesius & Griffith, 1996). To promote language and other emergent literacy development with children at risk or who exhibit language impairments, the facilitator needs to focus specifically on each child's behaviors and modify the reading to meet the child's emergent reading needs.

The following sections will discuss considerations for facilitating emergent reading development:

- General Principles for Facilitating Emergent Reading
- Specific Facilitation Strategies
- Transcripts of Reading Facilitation
- Reading Goals and Objectives

General Principles for Facilitating Emergent Reading

Reading with children should occur daily and can begin as early as birth. Reading the same book repeatedly helps the child internalize the story and develop early literacy skills, such as book orientation and print awareness. Facilitating behaviors of balancing interactions, matching the child's communicative level, responding to the child's verbal and nonverbal behaviors, being non-directive, and providing emotional attachment enhance the language and literacy-learning of adult-child reading episodes. Selecting books and engaging in storybook interactions appropriate to the developmental level of the child also are important for high-quality early reading experiences.

General Principles for Facilitating Emergent Reading

1. Engage in daily reading experiences.

2. Establish a reading routine.

3. Read the same book repeatedly.

4. Keep the reading child-focused and child-directed.

5. Select developmentally-appropriate books.

---

1. Daily Reading Experiences

Early and frequent adult-child book reading is one of the most important activities for facilitating a child's language and literacy development. Early reading experiences help children learn to attend to and discover the function of books and learn the literate language of written stories. Children who are read to and read with on a regular basis are better prepared to make the transition to conventional reading (Scarborough & Dobrich, 1994).

Reading to young children should be a daily activity. Regular reading experiences teach children that reading is valued and also show children how reading is important in their daily lives. Frequent and regular reading with young children is one of the most important adult-child activities associated with later academic success.

Although infants and toddlers lack the oral language skills to verbally interact with books, early encounters with books allow young children to begin making associations between objects and the illustrations in the book. At first, a child might randomly point to pictures, but with adult guidance and successive encounters with books, a child will purposefully point to a dog and later verbally label it.

As children gain verbal competence, they begin to label and comment on the pictures, but they lack enough knowledge about books to tell a coherent story (Sulzby, 1985). Frequent encounters with books, however, supported by a competent adult to scaffold the information, allow children to progress in reading development, including describing actions, using dialogue, and creating voices for characters. This progression is facilitated by adult reading partners who adjust the literacy demands and require children to provide increasingly more complex information about stories. Adults provide just enough verbal and visual support to enable children to be successful participants.

Through familiarity with books and reading, children learn to identify story information, relate it to their own experiences, and ultimately form stories with written language structures (Mason & Allen, 1986). Early reading episodes also provide children with the necessary precursors for conventional reading. Regular and frequent exposure to the symbols of print helps children learn how print communicates the stories in books. Adult-child storybook reading also offers children a foundation to begin mastering the conventions of reading (Yaden et al., 1989).

In summary, frequent early reading experiences allow children to sharpen, refine, and compare their own views of the world with new and unfamiliar information found in books.

2. Reading Routine

Routines are important to young children; they provide structure and develop familiarity for activities in the children's lives. Both aspects of routines, structure and familiarity, support children's learning and promote social-emotional well-being. Children who feel safe and secure are willing to take risks and actively explore the physical aspects of a familiar event. Establishing a regular reading routine provides children the needed opportunities to manipulate books, discover what they are, and learn how they are used.

For early reading routines to be most effective, the adult should maintain a conversational style. One routine found effective in promoting children's active reading participation is called a **Complete Reading Cycle (CRC)** (Crowe, 1996). The CRC is a four-step reading procedure based on a typical reading format (Ninio & Bruner, 1978). The four steps include a joint attentional focus, query, response, and feedback. A **joint attentional focus** establishes the topic to be discussed or read and to be shared between the adult and the child. The **query** includes questions and other techniques to elicit active, communicative turns from the child. The **response** serves as a reply to the query. **Feedback** acts to acknowledge, affirm, refute, or request clarification for the response.

The four steps are easily repeated throughout the storybook reading and, when mastered, facilitate a natural communicative exchange with the child.

It is important to embed interaction-promoting procedures, such as scaffolding, within the CRC to facilitate a child's active participation. Common scaffolding techniques include the following:

- Physical cues, such as pointing and gesturing

- Asking specific and nonspecific questions

- Giving partial utterances or responses

- Acknowledging, affirming, recasting or repeating, elaborating upon, or correcting children's communicative attempts

The information in the following section tells how the scaffolding techniques and strategies can be incorporated into a typical CRC.

Joint Attentional Focus

Joint attentional focus is established through verbal or nonverbal strategies that direct and maintain the child's attention to the story. These strategies include attentional vocatives, attentional gestures, and physical proximity.

- **Attentional vocatives** are verbalizations that direct and maintain the child's attention to the book or story, such as the following:

    "Look."

    "Look here."

    "See this."

    "Let's see what happens."

- **Attentional gestures** are nonverbal behaviors that direct and maintain the child's attention to the book or story by pointing to the people and objects, performing actions represented in the pictures or text, pointing to letters or words as the print is read or discussed, or pantomiming actions or events occurring in the story.

- **Physical proximity** refers to movement of the adult or book toward the child to direct and maintain attention to the story, including holding the book at the child's eye level, bringing the book to the child for the child to touch it, or moving physically closer to the child as the book is read.

Queries

Queries include verbal or nonverbal signals for the child to take a turn talking about the story. The purpose of the query is to get the child actively engaged in constructing the story so that the reading routine becomes more conversational. Queries can include a variety of questions or other eliciting techniques, including constituent questions, open-ended queries, and cloze procedures.

- **Constituent questions** are *wh-* questions that elicit specific information about the story, such as the following:

    "Who do you see?"

    "What is he/she doing?"

    "What is on his head?"

    "Where are they going?"

- **Open-ended queries** are questions or directives to elicit child-oriented verbalizations about the story. These include queries such as the following:

    "Tell me about this page."

    "What do you see?"

    "What's happening here?"

    These types of queries allow the adult to determine what the child does or doesn't know about the story and what information needs to be elaborated upon or explained.

- **Cloze procedures** are partial statements about the book or story that require the child to complete the utterance. A cloze procedure follows a fill-in-the-blank format, such as "He is getting ready to _____" and "There's a big _____." This procedure allows the child to participate in formulating a complete sentence when the child is not able to do so independently. It is particularly useful for children who are not yet combining words.

Responses

Responses are verbal and nonverbal communications by the child or adult that reply to a query. The adult may provide the verbal response when a query fails to elicit a response from the child.

- **Child verbal responses** include utterances produced by the child that have the syllabic structure and intonation pattern of a word, including minimal verbal responses, such as "Yes" and "Uh huh," and animal or environmental sounds that can be written as words, such as "Meow" and "Vroom."

- **Child nonverbal responses** are any gestures or other physical behaviors that provide a response to a query, such as pointing to the pictured items in the book, enacting a behavior shown in a picture, and facial expressions.

- **Adult verbal responses** include the target word or words the adult attempted to elicit through the query. The adult verbal response serves as a model for the child to imitate.

Feedback

Feedback includes additional verbal information from the adult or child that repeats, elaborates on, comments on the accuracy of, or acknowledges a response.

- **Repetitions** are partial or complete restatements of a preceding response, including repetition of the adult's own response or the child's response.

- **Elaborations** add information to the response. Elaborations also include providing the words for a child's nonverbal response; for example:

  Child: Pig.
  Adult: That's right, there's a little pig.

- **Corrections** are strategies to amend inaccurate information in the child's response, such as the following exchange:

  Child: Mad.
  Adult: Oh, I don't think he's mad. Look at his face. He's smiling. See how his mouth turns up? He must be happy.

Corrections may also include having the child imitate the amended response, such as the following:

  Child: Mad.
  Adult: Oh, I think he's happy. Look at his smiling, happy face. He's not mad; he's _____.

- **Acknowledgments** include comments such as "Okay" and "Uh huh" that acknowledge the child's response. However, acknowledgments alone may not strengthen the child's understanding. A repetition, an elaboration, or a correction can add more specific information to an acknowledgment.

The adult must continually fine-tune and adjust reading behaviors within this reading cycle to ensure the child's active participation (Whitehurst et al., 1988). Adult-child storybook reading should become a negotiation process that evolves and changes over time (Altwerger et al., 1985). Either the adult or the child can direct the other's attention to something of interest and ask questions about or comment on the people, objects, and events depicted. The adult should adjust the time spent in reading the text, asking questions, and commenting on the pictured information in response to the child's level of participation.

With repeated readings, repeated exposure to stories, and adult adjustments in reading behaviors, the child internalizes information about the story events and develops a greater understanding of the relationship between story and text. When the story or story structure become familiar and internalized, the child participates in retelling or partial reading of the story. As the child becomes familiar with the routine and with books, the child assumes the reader's role. The adult then provides the child with feedback that focuses on the meaning being shared to continually refine the child's reading behaviors.

Complete Reading Cycle

1. **Joint Attentional Focus**

   attentional vocative

   attentional gesture

   physical proximity

2. **Query**

   constituent question

   open-ended query

   cloze procedure

3. **Response**

   child verbal

   child nonverbal

   adult verbal

4. **Feedback**

   repetition

   elaboration

   correction

   acknowledgment

3. Repeated Reading

Repeatedly reading the same storybook is important for promoting children's literacy development. Multiple readings of a favorite storybook are associated with increases in children's attention, the use of de-contextualized language, and emergent reading behaviors (Kaderavek & Sulzby, 1998; Sulzby, 1985; Teale & Sulzby, 1986). Each new reading allows the child to learn something new. Interest in multiple readings is evident as a child asks for a favorite book to be read and reread daily. When the child internalizes relevant information from the story and no longer finds the story interesting or challenging, the child will find a new favorite story.

The pictures and text of storybooks are both stable and repeatable contexts that allow for learning more about a story across time. The same event can be talked about and referred to at different levels of language complexity and greater abstraction of meaning, such as moving from picture-focused to print-focused discussions (Norris, 1992). Whereas first readings may establish general information about the story, such as the characters, objects, actions, and simple events in the story, subsequent readings can build and elaborate on the characters and events. These elaborations can include attributes, such as size, shape, or color, and may facilitate generalization of pictured events to personal experiences.

Repeated readings also provide children opportunities to participate more fully in creating the story, retelling parts or predicting events that were remembered from the previous reading. To maintain the child's interest in the story and to increase the depth of understanding the child develops about the story, alter each reading in the following ways:

- Establish the relationships on the page by helping the child identify the people, objects, and actions. Reinforce these ideas by labeling the people, objects, and actions.

- Solidify the information from the previous reading by having the child retell elements of the story. Use open-ended questions to determine what the child does or does not know about the story, and frequently have the child summarize the events represented by the pictures or referred to in the text.

- Expand the information that has been established in the previous readings by including more detail and going beyond the pictures and text. This expansion can include developing unfamiliar vocabulary, referring to personal experiences, and asking questions that require more semantically-complex responses, such as *Why?* or *What will happen next?*

- Develop phonemic awareness naturally by directing the child's attention to the printed text. For example, do the following:

    Locate words or letters on the page.

    Find letters in the child's name.

Count words and letters.

Discuss long versus short words.

Ask the child to read the page.

Each successive reading allows the adult and child to talk about the same information with increasingly more literate language. By altering the focus of re-readings, the adult maintains the child's interest and promotes both oral and written language growth. The adult, however, adjusts the time spent reading the text, asking questions, and commenting on the pictured information in response to the child's advances in reading behaviors.

Through repeated readings, repeated exposure to stories, and adult adjustments in reading behaviors, the child internalizes information about the story events and develops a greater understanding of the relationship between the story and the text. When the story or story structure becomes familiar and internalized, the child participates in retelling, partial reading, and/or emergent reading of the story.

4. Child-Directed Reading

Active child participation is critical to maximize the learning opportunities of joint reading. The child's communicative and reading behaviors should dictate the facilitator's reading behaviors. The adaptations listed below should be embedded in joint reading experiences (MacDonald, 1989). Each adaptation is explained in more detail to follow.

Adaptations for Joint Reading Experiences

a. Balance facilitator-child interactions.

b. Match your behaviors to the child's level of participation.

c. Follow the child's lead.

d. Be non-directive.

e. Provide emotional attachment to boost the child's interest.

---

a. Balance facilitator-child interactions.

Give the child an equal number of turns, either by answering questions or by talking about, pointing to, and/or manipulating the book.

Allow the child to introduce topics or identify information that the child finds interesting.

Ask questions to determine what the child knows about the people, objects, or events in the pictures.

b. Match the child's participation.

Modify your behaviors to match the child's level of participation. If the child communicates through nonverbal actions, keep your comments short, action-oriented, and relevant to the pictures, such as "Oh, up" or "Ooh, jump."

Point to the pictures and actions associated with the words while making comments to maintain the child's attention to the information being shared.

c. Follow the child's lead.

When the child points to, touches, or talks about a picture, follow his or her movement or comment with an action or remark that tells the child something was communicated. For example, provide the words for the child's nonverbal actions, repeat the child's word or words, or rephrase the child's comment.

d. Be non-directive.

Avoid commanding or over-questioning the child. Persistent questions and commands place the child in a passive, respondent role and diminish the child's ability to actively explore and learn about the pictures and print.

Allow the child to tell what he or she already knows, and then follow the child's verbal or nonverbal turn by confirming, refuting, or adding to the child's information.

e. Provide emotional attachment.

During the reading experience, provide a motivating, risk-free environment that fosters the child's interest in exploring and reading books. An inviting social context ensures that the child will want to engage in reading over and over again.

Boost the child's interest in exploring and reading books by making the storybook reading meaningful and enjoyable for all participants.

5. Developmentally-Appropriate Books

Despite the numerous storybooks marketed for preschoolers, there are factors to consider in selecting a book that is developmentally appropriate for a young child. Selecting a book based on the publisher's or author's suggested age does not account for the child's developmental level. Therefore, select books that consider the communicative and conversational abilities exhibited by the child.

Preverbal Infants and Toddlers

Children at this stage of communicative and reading development view books as objects to manipulate (Norris, 1992). Children engage in sensorimotor exploration of books, such as chewing, dropping, and so on. As children emerge into purposeful nonverbal and early verbal communication, they will pat and point to familiar objects and begin to name some pictures. However, a book continues to be an object to explore.

There are many manipulable books designed for infant and toddler exploration. Sturdy books that can be chewed, banged, and handled in many different ways are ideal for the first storybook reading experiences. Touch-and-feel books, cloth books, and plastic books that picture one object per page are all appropriate for the first encounters with books.

Beginning Talkers

As children begin to use words more often than gestures to communicate, they also increase their understanding of stories and storybook reading. Children ask simple questions, make animal sounds and motor noises to comment on pictured information, and exhibit early book-handling skills, such as positioning a book right-side-up versus upside down (Monroe, 1969).

Beginning talkers at the one- or two-word level of communicative development respond well to books that show related items on a page, such as bath-time supplies, preschool toys, and meal items, or that illustrate single actions involving familiar events, such as washing, playing, and eating. These books may not have a sequential story, but they often represent individual story events on each page, such as brushing teeth, eating breakfast, and playing with toys. The stories should provide opportunities to expand on the child's emerging oral communicative development.

Conversational Readers

As children begin to combine words into sentences, they also begin to notice the connections between objects and actions represented in storybook pictures (Norris, 1992). While looking at books, these young conversationalists will comment "Doggie get bone" or "Mommy cook supper." These children also react to the emotions of the characters in the story, describing them as *happy* or *sad*. Children often want favorite storybooks read and reread until they have mastered the words and meanings (Monroe, 1969; Sulzby 1985).

Conversational children often recognize the storybook pictures as representations of objects and people engaged in ongoing actions. They also enjoy books that have a repeating phrase or theme. Books can include topics that are new or unfamiliar, such as fairy tales and make-believe stories. However, the words should describe or elaborate on what is happening in the pictures.

Beginning Readers

Through exposure to books and printed reading material and through interactive reading opportunities, children begin to notice letters and develop other print-awareness skills (Monroe, 1969; Sulzby, 1985). Children find capital letters in the text that correspond to the first letters in their names or to familiar environmental print. These children know that the printed word tells the reader what to say. Beginning readers are more focused on the words than on the pictures and will attend to short passages that have no corresponding pictures. Much of the language in favorite books is memorized and repeated or acted out in pretend play at other times of the day.

Children who know the connection between print and the ideas it conveys enjoy stories that allow them to participate in the reading. Books should depict a variety of actions, and there should be an overall plot, theme, or goal in the story. Many fairy tales and books with embedded story lines, such as Clifford books (Bridwell, 1972), are all appropriate for children at the beginning reader level.

Specific Facilitation Strategies

Common strategies for facilitating emergent reading include the following:

- Use physical cues, such as pointing and gesturing.

- Ask specific and nonspecific questions.

- Give partial utterances or responses.

- Acknowledge, affirm, recast or repeat, elaborate upon, or correct children's emergent reading attempts.

The following information describes facilitation techniques that can be incorporated into reading with children (Norris & Hoffman, 1993). The strategies are not presented in a developmental hierarchy but are presented in a manner to illustrate how to use the strategies with children at different levels of emergent reading.

Strategies to Facilitate Early Reading

1. **Focusing Strategies**
   Preparatory set
   Physical proximity
   Paraphrase

2. **Elicitation Strategies**
   Cloze procedure
   Gesture or pantomime
   Phonemic cue
   Binary choice question
   Constituent question
   Relational tie
   Semantic cue
   Comprehension or summarization question

3. **Feedback Strategies**
   Acknowledge or confirm
   Expand or reword
   Extend or link ideas
   Request clarification
   Negate and clarify

1. Focusing Strategies

Focusing strategies direct the child's attention to the book or pictures and are used to maintain the child's attention.

- **Preparatory set** establishes the topic, content, or focus of the reading. For example, point to pictures or say something to describe the event represented or to be read:

    "Look, a picnic!"

    "They're at the park."

    "Now they're picking berries."

- **Physical proximity** involves the position and use of the book in relation to the child. Here are some examples of using physical proximity to focus the child's attention on the reading:

    Bring the book to the child.

    Allow the child to reach out to the book.

    Hold the book easily within the child's view.

    Point to the pictures the story talks about.

    Point to words as you read them.

- **Paraphrase** or reword the text right after reading it.

2. Elicitation Strategies

Elicitation strategies help the child express what he or she understands about the story and are used to encourage the child's active participation in the reading.

- **Cloze procedure** provides a partial utterance with a fill-in-the-blank for the child to complete. Here are some examples:

    "Oh, look at the funny _____!" (Hold the book out for the child to touch.)

    "Oh, look at the funny _____. He has a big _____."

    "Big _____ . He looks really _____."

- Use **gestures** or **pantomime** to prompt the child's participation with nonverbal cues, such as points, touches, or reenactments. Some examples are listed on the next page.

Bounce the book up and down as you say, "See the clown jump."

Act out actions or expressions (e.g., smile, roll using hands).

Ask the child to act out or demonstrate pictured expressions.

- Give the child a **phonemic cue** by providing the initial sound or syllable of a word. Here are some examples:

  "That elephant is really /s/____." ("-ad," sad)

  "Look at his big / f /____." ("-eet," feet)

  "He doesn't have any /t/____." ("-oes," toes)

- Ask the child a **binary choice question**, a question that has two choices from which the child can select. Here are some examples:

  Label—"Is it a car or a truck?" "Do you see lions or tigers?"

  Describe—"Is he eating or drinking?"

  Interpret—"Is the clown happy or sad?"

  Predict—"Will he run away or stay?"

- Ask a **constituent question**, a question that asks the child for specific information. Here are some examples:

  "Who/What is that?"

  "Where are they going?"

  "What is he doing?"

- A **relational tie** indicates that more information is needed or elicits additional information with a cohesive tie. Here are some examples:

  Child: (touches the lion)
  Adult: Oh! Sharp teeth, and . . .
  Child: (touches the lion's tail)

  Child: The boy's eating popcorn.
  Adult: While . . .
  Child: He watches the clowns.

  Child: The lion is roaring.
  Adult: Because . . .
  Child: He's mad.

- Offer a **semantic cue** to define or give synonyms for words. Here are two examples for the word *tiny* in a story:

  "*Tiny.* That's another word for *little.*"

  "If something is really small, you could say it's _____."

- Ask a **comprehension** or a **summarization question** to check the child's understanding of all or parts of the story. In response, the child restates the information in his own words. Here are some examples:

  "Show me what Sammie is doing."

  "What did we find out about the clowns?"

  "What happened to Sammie?"

  "How does Sammie feel about losing the game?"

  "Why is Sammie mad?"

  "Tell me about the story we just read."

  "Remember this story? Read it to me."

3. Feedback Strategies

Feedback strategies follow a child's comment and acknowledge, add to, or refine the child's reading behaviors.

- **Acknowledge** or **confirm** that the reader's message was meaningful and understood without providing specific feedback. Here are some examples:

  "Yes."

  "You're right."

  "Okay."

- **Expand** or **reword** the child's comment using a more mature form of the remark, such as correct articulation or more complete/complex grammar. Here is an example:

  Child: (points to picture)
  Adult: Lion.
  Child: Lion.
  Adult: You're right. That is a lion.
  Child: Lion on chair.
  Adult: Yes, the lion is on the chair.

- **Extend** or **link** one idea of the story to the next idea or story. Here are some examples:

  Child: (points to picture)
  Adult: (points to the same picture) Yes, a lion in a cage.
         (points to another aspect of the picture)

  Child: There's a ball.
  Adult: Those kids are playing with the ball.

- **Request clarification** to help the child refine his or her message by showing, repeating, or rewording information that was not understood. Here are some examples:

  Child: (flips the pages of the book)
  Adult: Which page do you want to read?

  Child: There's a thing.
  Adult: Which thing?

  Child: It's a goobie.
  Adult: What's a goobie?

- **Negate and clarify** to let the child know when information is inaccurate and to help the child correct inaccuracies. (Note: Use negation cautiously; don't use it with children who are reluctant to participate.) Here are some examples:

  Child: (points to a cow) That's a dog.
  Adult: No, that's a cow. See, it has pointy horns and hooves.
         (points to and explains the parts of the cow; contrasts
         a cow with a dog, using a picture, if possible)

In summary, storybook reading is a natural adult-child activity that facilitates language and literacy development. Adult-child book-reading has an identifiable structure that unfolds in a conversational pattern that can be termed a **complete reading cycle** (Crowe, 1996). Within this routine, children learn a number of language and early reading skills as they actively participate in introducing topics, asking and answering questions, and giving feedback. Through repeated reading, child-focused interactions, and assistance from competent adult readers, children gain necessary precursors for conventional reading.

Transcripts of Reading Facilitation

The following examples illustrate the use of facilitation strategies during facilitator-child book-readings. Examples are presented in a developmental progression, with explanation and discussion provided. Keep in mind that children may exhibit characteristics at more than one stage, such as a beginning talker who understands and uses books at a preverbal level. Therefore, facilitator judgment is important in determining the types of facilitation to use.

Preverbal Level

The first example is a child at the preverbal level of emergent reading. The facilitator uses simple, short verbalizations. The pictures in the book are used as if they were real objects. For example, the facilitator models eating an apple pictured in the book. If the book contained a picture of a ball, the facilitator could bounce the book on the child's head, knees, hands, and so on while saying, "Boing" or "Bounce." After one or two bounces, the facilitator would stop and ask the child, "Now where?" or "More?" The facilitator would watch to see how the child responds and give the child a chance to touch her head or knee or to hold out a hand.

Any little movement or verbalization can be turned into a communication. The facilitator's verbalizations are simple and focused on the objects in the pictures. The facilitator keeps the child actively involved by providing opportunities for the child to point to things she recognizes. The child's nonverbal and verbal communicative attempts are expanded into more mature forms.

Reading Exchange: Nonverbal Child

The facilitator and Gretchen are looking at a book containing a picture of an apple. Throughout the book exchange, the facilitator balances turns, models behaviors for Gretchen, follows Gretchen's lead, adds semantically contingent information, and ensures Gretchen's active participation.

Gretchen: (grabs the book and chews it)

Gretchen's book knowledge is at the earliest developmental stage. She understands books as objects to be mouthed and chewed. She also indicates that the book must be brought to her. She is not reaching out to touch things in the book. Instead she brings the book to her body; in this instance, her mouth. The facilitator takes this opportunity to build upon Gretchen's emergent reading knowledge and then expands and models more complex reading behaviors.

continued on next page

Facilitator: (expands) Oh, apple. Yum.
(pantomimes, using the book as an object; pretends to take a bite, then gives the book back to Gretchen to imitate the behavior)

Gretchen: Mmm. (chews book)

Gretchen now vocalizes as she continues to use the book as an object for sensorimotor exploration. The facilitator again expands upon Gretchen's behaviors, waits to see how she responds, and keeps the interaction going.

Facilitator: (expands) Mmm, good. Juicy.
(uses a turn-taking cue) More?
(waits to see how Gretchen responds to the question)

Gretchen: Gah.

The facilitator uses physical and verbal strategies to elicit verbal turns from Gretchen. As the facilitator expands Gretchen's vocalizations into real words, such as interpreting and expanding *gah* to *good*, the facilitator maintains a short utterance length to stay within Gretchen's ZPD (see page 7).

Facilitator: (acknowledges and expands) Yes, good apple.

Beginning Talker

This second example is a child just beginning to use identifiable words. At this level of storybook reading, it is important for the facilitator to model lots of things for the child to say and then give the child opportunities to talk about what he sees. Together the facilitator and child jointly construct the story by each taking turns to talk about the people, objects, or actions illustrated on the pages. The facilitator does not read the text, but uses objects or props to act out parts of the story. Reading portions of the text may be added later once the child is familiar with the action or events in the story. The facilitator ensures that any words that are read match the pictures on the page.

Throughout this joint reading episode, the facilitator continually provides information and feedback that facilitate the child's grasp of concepts about books and print. The facilitator observes and responds to the child's reading behaviors. The facilitator models more mature verbal forms, but doesn't ask the child to correct his productions. That is, the facilitator focuses more on *what* the child says than on *how* he says it. Then the facilitator provides information to create a more meaningful, complete communicative exchange.

Reading Exchange: Beginning Talker

Emilio and the facilitator are reading a story about a picnic. Props for the story include a picnic basket and things to go in the basket, such as foods and dishes. The facilitator first talks about the pictured information, then uses the props to review and solidify the ideas illustrated in the story.

Emilio is a beginning talker who displays intentional communicative behaviors. He is beginning to connect the pictures to objects in the real world, so he asks a question about something that is new or unfamiliar.

    Emilio: Dat? (points to picture)

By allowing Emilio to initiate a topic, the facilitator can now elaborate on his topic of interest, maintaining a child-oriented exchange. First, the facilitator responds to Emilio's question. Next, the facilitator points and verbally directs Emilio's attention to related information, helping Emilio connect the objects in the story. Offering this visual information also facilitates Emilio's ability to actively contribute to the story construction.

    Facilitator: (expands) Oh, a basket.
                (provides a preparatory set) Look.
                (points to the picture and adds a cloze procedure) Mommy's putting in ____. (points to the picture of what the child can talk about)

Emilio responds with an early production of *apple*. Instead of asking Emilio to correct his production, the facilitator focuses on the content of Emilio's information. The facilitator's short utterance adds to Emilio's understanding of the important information depicted in the pictures, using words that focus on the most salient objects in the picture that contribute to the story line (the items that go in the picnic basket). The facilitator is careful to avoid utterances that focus on irrelevant information that doesn't contribute to the event depicted on the page, such as the sink in the kitchen, pictures on the walls, etc.

    Emilio: Appo.

    Facilitator: (affirms and expands) That's right. Apples.
                (adds a relational tie to request more information)
                And ____ (points to another pictured object for Emilio to name)

Following the facilitator's relational tie, Emilio responds with another label.

    Emilio: Cookie.

continued on next page

Now the facilitator can add a description of the cookies that expands the semantic information related to what Emilio said. The facilitator continues with Emilio's idea before providing additional information relevant to the story.

Facilitator: (elaborates) Yes, CHOC-O-LATE (emphasis) cookies.
(adds a relational tie to request more information) And . . . ?
(waits for Emilio to say something)

Note that the facilitator did not point this time, but verbally requested more information and waited to see if Emilio could continue adding information about the foods to go in the picnic basket.

Emilio: (no response)

Emilio was unable to provide another idea without a visual cue or a more specific verbal facilitation strategy, such as a binary choice question. To maintain Emilio's active participation, the facilitator could either provide the requested information or try another strategy to assist Emilio in continuing with the story. A more-direct question accompanied by a point provides a sufficient scaffold to facilitate Emilio's turn.

Facilitator: (provides a turn-taking cue) Anything else?
(points to the dishes beside the basket)

Emilio: Pate.

The facilitator can now refine Emilio's response and continue to add more information about the event. The facilitator continues to elicit information that closely matches Emilio's developmental level (primarily labels), but the facilitator now uses the props to provide Emilio the physical experience associated with the story, thereby establishing the connection between the pictured and real objects. This re-enactment adds cohesion to the overall story by putting together the parts of the event, such as actions and objects within the event.

Facilitator: (affirms and expands) Yes, plates.
(provides a preparatory set) Let's help put the food in the basket.
(adds a cloze procedure) Put in the ____.
(pauses and waits for Emilio to put food in the basket)

Emilio provides the label as he acts out the story events. This reenactment makes explicit much of the implied information that occurs in the story and that is not represented pictorially, such as how the food gets into the basket.

continued on next page

> Emilio: Cookie. (puts the cookie in the basket)
>
> Next the facilitator reviews and repeats the story that has already been discussed. Using the props and slightly altering the activity keeps the repetition from becoming stilted or drill-like. Instead, the facilitator and Emilio continue to be balanced conversational partners, with the facilitator frequently restating and expanding Emilio's utterances.
>
> > Facilitator: (restates and uses a cloze procedure) Cookie and the ____. (pause)
>
> > Emilio: Appo. (puts the apple in the basket)
>
> Note that Emilio provides a response without the facilitator using a point or gesture. This progress is accomplished through Emilio's active participation during the initial discussion about the illustrations. New information can now be added as Emilio has demonstrated understanding of the story to this point. The facilitator models additional information to develop concepts about the topic. That is, apples are more than just objects; they are good things to eat. Descriptions of how the apple might taste are added, and other pragmatic functions that might be found in storybook text are demonstrated.
>
> > Facilitator: (expands and extends) Apple. Yum, yum. I want some.
>
> The facilitator's additional information elicits a question/request from Emilio.
>
> > Emilio: Me? (points to self)
>
> > Facilitator: (affirms and expands) Yes, you may have some, too.
>
> Emilio thus exhibits a shift in his storybook reading behaviors, demonstrating an emotional response to what is occurring. As Emilio uses more advanced reading behaviors, the facilitator can continue to model and request more complex semantic information and varied pragmatic functions.

Conversational Level

The child in this example demonstrates reading at a conversational stage of emergent reading development. She follows the story action, understands familiar action sequences represented in the pictures or described in the text, and enjoys being read to as well as participating in the story construction.

This is the third reading of the book, so the facilitator will require the child to contribute what she already knows about the story. During the first reading, the facilitator pointed to the pictures while reading the words and provided literate-language statements, such as *It says here* and *Let's see what the words say.* The child participated less during the first reading, but listened intently and asked questions about new or unfamiliar information. Subsequent readings now focus on joint reading of the story.

Reading Exchange: Conversational Level

Lily and the facilitator are reading a familiar story. The facilitator checks Lily's comprehension to see what she remembers from the previous readings and also uses literate language, such as the word *story*, to facilitate Lily's knowledge of written language. Lily's reading behaviors show evidence of both oral and literate language characteristics. She is beginning to make the oral-to-literate transition, important for more-advanced reading development.

Throughout this example, the facilitator does the following:

- integrates focusing, eliciting, and feedback strategies within each reading turn

- analyzes each of Lily's reading behaviors

- acknowledges what Lily says

- expands or extends Lily's reading into a complete or more elaborate idea

- elicits more information from Lily

Although Lily is familiar with the people, objects, and actions represented in the pictures, she does not independently combine this information into a meaningful event. Her reading is primarily picture-governed; she talks about the pictured people, objects, and actions. Elements of print-governed reading are emerging, such as using the text words she remembers to comment on the pictured information. The facilitator embeds text words and paraphrases text into the verbal exchanges. This embedding may include paraphrases, such as "but he remembered to" when the text reads *I didn't forget to.* This facilitation enhances Lily's understanding of the story structure and promotes her emergent reading development.

continued on next page

The facilitator begins with a simple *yes/no* question that provides a preparatory set about the book and also checks Lily's comprehension of the familiar story.

Facilitator: (checks comprehension) Okay, do you know this story?

Although the facilitator asks a *yes/no* question, Lily's familiarity with the story allows her to respond with a complete sentence. She also includes literate language, part of the book title, in her response.

Lily: Yeah, it's *Just Forgot*.

Now the facilitator checks to see how much of the literate language and print awareness Lily has internalized about the story. The facilitator's comprehension question is open-ended and provides no prompt or cue to elicit specific information about the story.

Facilitator: (affirms and expands) That's right, *I Just Forgot*.
(asks comprehension question) Can you read the story to me?

The facilitator continues with this less-supportive approach until Lily is unable to retell critical aspects of the story independently.

Lily: Well, Critter can't remember.

The facilitator's question elicits a repeating theme of the story. Lily's reading response contains elements of a contextually-dependent oral narrative, but Lily doesn't provide the main idea expressed on the page, *forgetting to make the bed.* The facilitator uses what Lily already knows and expands it by scaffolding Lily through the event relationships, which are people and objects performing actions. The facilitation strategies direct Lily's attention to important information she needs in her narrative.

Because Lily cannot recall the more-specific elements of the story, the facilitator uses strategies that provide both visual and verbal support, attending to her responses and adjusting the facilitation strategies according to her needs.

Facilitator: (provides a relational tie) Remember to . . .
(adds visual support with a point; pauses and points to pictures that follow the action in the story)

continued on next page

Adding the visual cue of pointing to the picture allows Lily to follow the action in the story, facilitating her comprehension of the complete ideas expressed on the page, such as *Critter forgot to make the bed,* versus events containing incomplete or nonspecific information, such as *He forgot.*

Lily: Make the bed.

The facilitator continues using the same strategies of acknowledging/affirming, verbally prompting, and visually cueing with a point to assist Lily's reading of the pictures in the story.

Facilitator: (affirms, extends, and provides a relational tie) Yes, but he remembered to . . . (pauses and points to the pictures)

Lily: Brush his teeth.

Lily readily provides the action sequences of the story. The facilitator takes note of these behaviors and again withdraws some of the more specific support, the visual cue. Instead, the next few turn-taking exchanges highlight the equal contributions of Lily and the facilitator to the story construction.

Facilitator: (affirms and adds a relational tie) That's right, he didn't . . . (pauses)

Lily: Forget.

Facilitator: (extends) To brush his teeth.
              (adds a relational tie) He just forgot . . . (pauses)

Lily: His bed.

Beginning Reader

This last example is a beginning reader who demonstrates print-focused reading behaviors. While the child has good grapho-phonemic knowledge, he often creates non-words as he reads because he focuses more on decoding the words than having a meaningful communicative exchange with the author. The facilitator uses strategies that "push" meaning into the reading, including the following:

- Frequently point from the pictures to the printed words.

- Give the child clues about the text passage before reading.

- Comment on the meaning expressed by what the child reads.

The facilitator embeds questions and comments in a conversational style throughout the reading of the passage.

Reading Exchange: Beginning Reader

The facilitator and Nickolai are reading *Clifford the Small Red Puppy* (Bridwell, 1972). The text on page one reads *Hi! I'm Emily Elizabeth and this is Clifford, my big red dog.*

Facilitator:	(focuses attention) Look, (points to picture) this is Emily Elizabeth (points to name in the text).
	(provides preparatory set) She's going to tell us about her dog, Clifford.
Nickolai:	Hi. I'm Emily Elizabeth.
Facilitator:	(affirms and provides preparatory set) That is Emily Elizabeth. And now she's going to tell us her dog's name.
Nickolai:	And this is my dog, Clifford, my dog, my big red dog.

Nickolai was anticipating a different word order after the facilitator's preparatory set. His surprise resulted in a maze, nonfluent reading that included a false start and repetitions. Before continuing to the next page, the facilitator has him reread the page to familiarize himself with the characters' names.

Facilitator:	(provides expansion and points to text) Clifford is a really big, red dog.
	(elaborates and provides additional meaning) He's much bigger than (points to text) Emily Elizabeth.
	(checks comprehension) Now, what was Emily Elizabeth telling us again?
Nickolai:	That her dog's name is Clifford.
Facilitator:	(affirms and requests rereading of the text) Yes, the dog's name is Clifford. Read and find out what else she told us about Clifford.
Nickolai:	(reads) Hi! I'm Emily Elizabeth and this is Clifford, my big red dog.

continued on next page

After reading the first page, Nickolai turns to the second page. The facilitator and Nickolai could elaborate and extend the reading by talking about their own pets and how they compare to Clifford. Instead, they choose to continue reading the story.

On the second page, the text reads *Yesterday my friend Martha said, "I got my dog from a fancy pet store. Where did you get yours?"*

Because there are multiple lines of text and several ideas expressed within the passage, the facilitator will have Nickolai read small portions. This technique is called **parsing**. Parsing allows the beginning reader to comprehend ideas that may be separated by embedded clauses or temporal markers.

Facilitator:	(directs attention and provides a preparatory set) Look. (points to picture) Here's another girl with Emily Elizabeth. She has a big dog, too.
Nickolai:	Yeah, but he's not as big as Clifford.
Facilitator:	(affirms and elaborates) No, Clifford is much bigger than this brown dog. (provides a preparatory set) I wonder what the girl's name is. Can you find it in this line? (points to first line of text)

The facilitator checks to see if Nickolai understands and uses capitalization cues to locate the proper noun (girl's name) in the text.

Nickolai:	(points to the word *Martha*) Here it is. Mar-tee-uh, Martia.

The facilitator did not ask Nickolai to read the name, only to find it. Because Nickolai attempted to pronounce the word, the facilitator now gives him feedback about the word.

Facilitator:	(affirms) You did find the girl's name. And it does look like *Martia*. But the *TH* in the middle makes my mouth want to say *Martha*. Martha is telling Emily Elizabeth where she got her dog. (checks comprehension) Where do you think Martha got her dog?
Nickolai:	On a farm or from a friend.

continued on next page

Facilitator: (affirms and elaborates) Those are both good places to get dogs. These words (points to *pet store*) tell us where Martha got her dog.

Nickolai: Pet shop, store.

At first Nickolai anticipated the word would be *shop,* but he used his grapho-phonemic knowledge to self-correct the word.

Facilitator: (affirms and repeats) Yes, Martha got her dog at a pet store.
(points to text) And it wasn't a plain, old pet store, it was all decorated really . . . (points to text to be read)

Nickolai: Fancy.

Facilitator: (affirms and repeats; points to text) It was a fancy pet store.

The facilitator has established where Martha got her dog and helped Nickolai decode any potentially difficult words in the sentence. Now the facilitator has Nickolai read the entire sentence to check the effectiveness of the cues that have been used.

Facilitator: (points to text to be read) Read and find out what Martha told Emily Elizabeth.

Nickolai: I got my dog from a fancy pet store.

Facilitator: (affirms and summarizes) So, Martha got her dog at a fancy pet store.
(provides a preparatory set) Now she wants to know where Emily Elizabeth got her dog. Read what Martha asks Emily Elizabeth.

Nickolai: When did you get yours?

Facilitator: (negates and provides a visual cue by pointing to the text) Martha didn't want to know **when,** she wanted to find out _____. (points to text)

Nickolai: Where?

continued on next page

Facilitator: (affirms and repeats) Yeah, Martha wants to know where Emily Elizabeth got Clifford.

The facilitator either negates or affirms what Nickolai reads. The facilitator also repeats, elaborates, or requests clarification to help Nickolai realize that reading should be a meaningful interaction.

Facilitator: (does a quick comprehension check using a cloze procedure) Well, Emily Elizabeth and Martha are talking about _____.

Nickolai: Their dogs.

Facilitator: (affirms and uses another cloze procedure) That's right. And Martha told Emily Elizabeth _____.

Nickolai: That she got her dog at a pet store.

Facilitator: (requests more information) Anything else?

Nickolai: Martha wants to know where she got Clifford.

Facilitator: (affirms and summarizes) That's right. Martha wants to know where Emily Elizabeth got her dog, Clifford.

Now the facilitator goes back to establish the time when the conversation occurred. The facilitator could have established the time frame earlier, but chose to first focus on the conversation between Emily Elizabeth and Martha.

Facilitator: (summarizes and provides a preparatory set) Well, Emily Elizabeth and Martha are talking about their dogs, but they didn't talk about them today. They were talking before today. This word tells us when they talked about their dogs.

Nickolai: Yesterday.

Facilitator: (affirms and elaborates) Yes, they talked about their dogs yesterday.
(provides a preparatory set and a cloze procedure) And this tells us that Martha and Emily Elizabeth really like each other. Martha is Emily Elizabeth's _____.

continued on next page

Nickolai: Friend.

Facilitator: (summarizes and then requests that the entire passage be read) So, Emily Elizabeth is telling us about a talk with her friend Martha. Read and find out what Emily Elizabeth said.

Nickolai: Yesterday my friend Martha said, "I got my dog from a funny, fancy pet store. Where did you get yours?"

Throughout this facilitated reading, the facilitator provides numerous visual and verbal cues to establish the ideas and to prevent Nickolai from miscuing (i.e., misreading the words). Because Nickolai relies on a grapho-phonemic strategy for reading, the facilitator helps Nickolai use multiple reading cues prior to, during, and after reading. This assistance helps Nickolai to understand what he reads and to read with greater fluency and accuracy.

Reading Goals and Objectives

Object-Focused, Preverbal Child

Goal: The child will interact with books at increasing levels of displacement.

Objectives: The child will:

- Explore the book by mouthing, banging, chewing, etc.

- Reach out to touch the book, flip through the pages, and/or look at the pictures.

Picture-Focused, Beginning Talker

Goal: The child will use picture-based behaviors to participate in storybook reading.

Objectives: The child will:

- Listen to developmentally-appropriate stories read by adults for three-to-five minutes.

- Demonstrate correct book orientation.

- Point to and/or name pictures in books.

- Ask simple questions relevant to the story, such as *what, who,* and *where* questions.

- Describe or state the action of the story events.

- Repeat familiar story lines or rhyming parts of stories, either independently or with a prompt.

Picture-Focused Conversationalist

Goal: The child will express story-related ideas pictured in a familiar book.

Objectives: The child will:

• Talk to and/or react to characters and actions pictured in a book.

• Predict past and future events relevant to a familiar story.

• Use an oral narrative style to tell parts of a story.

• Make print-related comments, such as *Just read the words.*

• Point to and/or name familiar letters spontaneously or when prompted.

• Use a literate language style to tell part or all of a story.

• Demonstrate word segmentation by pointing to each word while pretending to read a story.

Print-Focused, Beginning Reader

Goal: The child will read, retell, and/or talk about simple stories.

Objectives: The child will:

• Read portions of text using multiple sources, such as picture clues, grapho-phonemic associations, sentence structure, and background information.

• Read a story, and then demonstrate comprehension by answering simple questions about the story, such as *who, what,* and *where* questions.

• Read a developmentally-appropriate passage or story fluently.

• Read a developmentally-appropriate passage or story with appropriate phrasing and intonation.

With the wave of an infant's fist, the writing process has begun for the child. This may seem an odd statement to make to many people, yet Vygotsky (1962) suggests that writing begins as gestures in the air.

People interpret an infant's reflexive arm movements and other unintentional gestures as meaningful communication: "Look, he's waving to you." Through these social responses, babies soon learn that gestures, like the vocal sounds they produce, have power.

This chapter will trace the development of writing in young children from that first innocent gesture, through drawing to represent knowledge, and finally to conventional symbols of writing.

Young children develop concepts about writing long before they produce conventional writing. These concepts are developed through children's daily immersion in a print-rich environment.

- There is writing on their clothes and on their toys.

- There is writing in their parents' newspapers and in their own favorite storybooks.

In addition to hearing the written words that others read, children see writing being used for real purposes.

- The shopping list is written before leaving for the market.

- Phone messages are recorded on paper.

- Post-it notes serve as reminders to pay the water bill and pick up the dry cleaning.

Through natural interactions with competent readers and writers, children develop ideas about the function and form of written language.

Stages of Drawing Development

As with gestures, the physical process of writing typically does not begin through an intentional act.

Twelve-month-old Sherese reaches for the shiny object on the table and waves it around, leaving behind a mark on the tablecloth. She notices the mark. Fascinated by the mark, she moves her hand again and again. Her writing attempts meet with inconsistent success as Sherese has yet to realize that marks appear only when the tip of the pen touches the tablecloth. Sherese and other children her age enjoy not only the visual aspects of writing, but the kinesthetic experience as well (Harrison, 1999).

Children draw to represent their world. As they acquire more knowledge and a better understanding of their world, their drawing changes. This change or development in drawing typically occurs in a predictable sequence (Harrison, 1999) using a set of graphic principles (Wilson & Wilson, 1982). The first stage in the development of drawing is referred to as the **manipulative** (Gaitskellet et al., 1982) or **scribbling stage** (Linderman & Herberholz, 1972). This stage typically occurs from two-to-four years of age. In the initial phase of this stage, children derive pleasure from simply "leaving their mark." They make no attempt to use marks as meaningful symbols. Through scribbling, however, children develop a repertoire of lines and marks that they will use in future symbolic drawings. Near the end of this stage, children often verbalize while drawing (Harrison, 1999). The drawings typically bear little, if any, resemblance to the children's narratives. By labeling the objects, children demonstrate a rudimentary understanding that visual marks can represent meaning.

The **symbolic stage** of development begins around age four and is typically completed by age eight (Lowenfeld & Brittain, 1987). During this stage, children progress from using crude circular and linear forms that may represent any number of objects to drawing detailed human figures (Harrison, 1999). Initial human figures may consist of a circle with two dots for the eyes. By the end of the stage, human figures include feet, hands, fingers, and noses. Improvement in representing objects also occurs, so the drawings look more like the intended objects. In addition to these changes, children in the symbolic stage demonstrate a better understanding of space. For example, they establish relationships between people and objects by where the figures are placed on the paper. Also, a ground line may appear so that people no longer seem to be floating in space (Harrison, 1999).

These increases in symbolic representation enable children to communicate greater meaning via graphic symbols.

In the final stage of development, the **schematic** or **pre-adolescent stage**, children use drawings to depict clear relationships between people and objects, including character perspective. Most children enter this stage between eight and nine years of age. Because this stage begins after the preschool years, further discussion of this stage is not within the scope of this book.

Principles of Drawing

Within the global stages of drawing development just described, Wilson and Wilson (1982) identified seven graphic principles that children employ in their drawings. One or several of these principles may be applied to a single drawing, but not all children use all of the principles, and the principles may be applied differently at different levels of development. These individual variations in use of the graphic principles within and across developmental stages make it extremely difficult to identify an exact continuum of drawing development.

Principles of Drawing

1. Simplicity principle

2. Perpendicular principle

3. Territorial-imperative principle

4. Fill-the-format principle

5. Conservation multiple-application principle

6. Draw-everything principle

7. Plastic principle

1. Simplicity Principle

The simplicity principle is the most basic of the seven principles. In essence, children operating under this principle will depict an object in the simplest manner possible. A circle may suffice as a representation of a person. Simple depictions are common for very young children as they are just beginning to develop their understanding of objects, although the principle is applied by adult artists as well (Wilson & Wilson, 1982).

2. Perpendicular Principle

Contrast is the key to the perpendicular principle. Drawings influenced by this principle demonstrate a significant contrast among parts of objects. The horizontal and vertical lines of ladders represent an early example of this principle.

3. Territorial-Imperative Principle

The territorial-imperative principle assigns each object in the drawing its own space. Overlap in figures or objects is not allowed. For example, a child draws a girl with long hair that extends beyond the shoulders. If the hair is drawn first, arms will be omitted because the arms and hair cannot overlap.

4. Fill-the-Format Principle

The fill-the-format principle prompts children to fill all the available space provided. Filling every inch of the paper may result in extra legs for the cow because there is room for leg number five. Perhaps the body of the dog is drawn too small to accommodate four legs, so only two are included.

5. Conservation and Multiple-Application Principle

The conservation and multiple-application principle capitalizes on children's limited drawing skills. For example, human heads are used for horses and cats, and the sun is recycled as hands and feet (Wilson & Wilson, 1982).

6. Draw-Everything Principle

In the draw-everything principle, multiple perspectives are included in a single drawing. People are shown with clothes on, although the belly button can be seen. Pictures simultaneously show the inside and the outside of a house, or a chair is drawn from a top and side view.

7. Plastic Principle

Drawings influenced by the plastic principle reveal which people, objects, or actions are most important to the child. Under this principle, the most important element of the drawing is exaggerated. For example, in a family picture, children may draw themselves larger than their parents.

The general stages in drawing development and the principles of drawing described above outline how children come to represent or symbolize their understanding of their world. Through experience with drawing, children come to realize that ideas and spoken words can be expressed through visual symbols. This understanding is essential for the development of conventional writing.

Conventional Writing

Each morning, as he waited for the other children to arrive, four-year-old Jeff pulled his favorite book from the shelf and carried it to one of the preschool teachers to read with him. Each morning the teacher read Blue Sea *(Kalan, 1992) with him, talking about the pictures and pointing out the printed words. Jeff loved the story about how the little fish escaped being eaten by the big fish. He would say the words that the little fish said, "Bye-bye, big fish," as he swam to safety, but Jeff didn't understand that the words printed on the page told the teacher what the little fish said.*

The preschool teacher continued to read the story with Jeff each morning, talking about the action and running her finger under the words to show Jeff what the little fish said. One morning, as the teacher and Jeff read Blue Sea *yet one more time, Jeff pointed to the printed words as he said, "Bye-bye, big fish." The connection had been made. Jeff now understood that the printed words told the story.*

Conventional writing is often viewed in terms of spelling. However, even before children like Jeff develop a conscious awareness that spoken words can be written down and that it is the printed words that tell the story, children have been experimenting with and producing writing (Snow et al., 1998; Sulzby et al., 1989). To achieve conventional spelling, children must develop an understanding of the **alphabetic principle**, the systematic relationship between letters and sounds (Adams, 1990). In English, however, letters do not map to sounds in a direct one-to-one correspondence. This feature of English adds to the child's challenge in learning to spell.

Research in beginning writing has identified a developmental progression that begins as scribbles and ends with conventional spelling (Ferreiro, 1986; Gentry, 1982; Henderson & Beers, 1980; Read, 1971; Teale & Sulzby, 1986; Sulzby et al., 1989).

Sulzby and her colleagues (1989) identified two forms of scribbling, wavy and letter-like. **Wavy scribbles** are characterized by a continuous line without any forms that resemble letters.

Letter-like scribbling includes writing that has some features of letters. Unlike wavy scribbles, letter-like scribbles exhibit variations in form as a result of motor control. For example, a letter-like scribble may include a reversal in the direction of a loop or a descending line such as one used in a lower-case letter *y*.

As writing becomes more conventional, letters begin to appear. Typical stages of spelling development are listed on page 68. Progression through these stages of development is not age specific, but rather is influenced by a child's literacy experiences.

Stages of Spelling Development

There are seven stages children progress through as they develop spelling skills.

Stages of Spelling Development

1. Pre-phonemic stage
2. Early phonemic stage
3. Letter-name stage
4. Semi-phonetic stage
5. Phonetic stage
6. Transitional stage
7. Conventional stage

1. Pre-Phonemic Stage

Spelling at the pre-phonemic stage consists of a string of random letters. At this stage of development, a child's spelling may also include number symbols as part of the writing. Some knowledge of the alphabetic principle is demonstrated through the use of letters; however, knowledge of letter/sound correspondence is not evidenced at this stage (Gentry, 1982).

MNY EFAN Γ6Σξ

2. Early Phonemic Stage

At the early phonemic stage of development, the child demonstrates a rudimentary knowledge of letter/sound correspondence. Words are spelled with appropriate beginning letters, but random letters are used to represent the remainder of the word. The following example could be *play* or *paint*.

PoAH

3. Letter-Name Stage

At the letter name stage of spelling, the names of letters are used to represent a syllable. To spell the words *Alex* and *empty*, the child would only need to write *LX* and *MT* as in the examples below. Although far from conventional spelling, this stage demonstrates growth in the child's understanding of letter/sound correspondence.

LX   MT

4. Semi-Phonetic Stage

Spelling at the semi-phonetic stage of development is characterized by an increase in the number of sounds represented by letters. Not all sounds or syllables of a word are represented, though, as in *spaghetti, doctor,* and *Goldilocks* below.

speget   dotr   gloks

5. Phonetic Stage

At the phonetic stage, letters are used to represent all the sounds in a word (Gentry, 1982; Read, 1975). The choice of letters is based strictly on the sounds perceived, so some letter choices or sequences of letters may be unconventional, but perceptually correct. The words *wondering* and *smart* could be written as follows:

wodring   smrt

6. Transitional Spelling Stage

The transitional spelling stage occurs as children become more aware of the conventions of English spelling. Children incorporate more orthographic principles into their spelling (Gentry, 1982), as illustrated in *enough* and *train* below. Each syllable is marked by a vowel and various spelling patterns. At this stage, children often write words they already know how to spell rather than attempting unfamiliar words.

enogh   trane

7. Conventional Spelling

The last stage is conventional spelling. At this stage, a child's knowledge of English orthography is firmly established. The child accurately spells words with prefixes and suffixes; words with uncommon spelling patterns, such as *ie*; and words with irregular spellings. Although children at this stage don't spell all words accurately, they have a large corpus of words that they can spell correctly.

money   said

Learning to write, like learning to speak, is a complex developmental process. Children's transition from one stage of writing to the next is gradual. A single sample of writing may include writing elements characteristic of more than one stage, although children do not regress back to an earlier stage once a higher, more refined level has been firmly attained.

Early Writing Checklist

The Early Writing Checklist on pages 71-72 provides a guide for professionals to identify a young child's understanding and use of writing. The checklist is arranged to reflect a general progression in writing development, and it includes some of the distinguishing behaviors children exhibit in the areas of drawing and spelling.

Completing the Early Writing Checklist requires collecting a writing sample, which may be a drawing only, writing only, or a drawing with writing. The sample may be collected in either a group or an individual setting. Give the child a sheet of paper and a pencil and ask the child to write a story. Provide ample time and encouragement for the child to complete the writing. Always ask the child to put his or her name on the paper. If the child is unable to or does not write the date independently, the professional who collects the sample should date the paper.

Note whether the writing was about a topic **familiar** to the child, such as a story that had been read together, an event picture that had been discussed, or a trip to the zoo; or an **unfamiliar** topic, such as a picture that the child has not seen before. Additionally, note whether the written sample was completed independently or with assistance. If assistance was provided, describe that assistance in the comments section.

Early Writing Checklist

Child's name _____ Age _____

Writing topic _____ Date _____

Recorder _____ Setting _____

Sample completed: Independently   With assistance
(Circle one.)

Topic: Familiar   Unfamiliar
(Circle one.)

Check all listed or similar behaviors observed. Note similar behaviors beside those listed. Comment below on other factors that influenced the writing, such as the child's inattention, environmental factors, writing materials, etc.

Drawing Development: Form

_____ makes undirected marks on paper (unintentional)

_____ makes directed marks on paper (intentional)

_____ names unrecognizable scribble after it is drawn

_____ names unrecognizable scribble while drawing (several distinct scribbles present)

_____ draws crude objects or human figures

_____ produces drawings that begin to resemble intended figures/objects

_____ positions figures/objects in space to establish relationships

Drawing Development: Function

_____ uses picture to tell the entire story (no writing)

_____ embeds pictures with other forms of writing

_____ uses drawing as illustration only; tells story through writing

Writing/Spelling Development

_____ produces wavy scribbling

_____ produces letter-like scribbling

_____ uses random letter strings; may include numbers (pre-phonemic stage)

_____ uses appropriate beginning letters followed by random letters (early phonemic stage)

_____ uses letter name to spell syllables (letter-name stage)

_____ uses letters to represent some but not all sounds and/or syllables (semi-phonetic stage)

_____ uses letters to represent all sounds of word but spelling is unconventional (phonetic stage)

_____ uses spelling that is more conventional (transitional stage)

_____ spells words correctly (conventional stage)

Basic Concepts of Print

_____ demonstrates left-to-right progression

_____ demonstrates top-to-bottom progression

_____ uses print to tell the story

_____ puts space between words

_____ demonstrates one-to-one correspondence between spoken and written words

Comments

_____

_____

_____

Note: Based on Clay (1975); Norris (1999a); Sulzby, Barhart, & Hieshima (1989); with adaptations from Gentry, J. R. (1982). An analysis of developmental spelling in GYNS at WRK. *The Reading Teacher, 36,* 192-200. Reprinted with permission of J. Richard Gentry and the International Reading Association. All rights reserved.

Chapter 5: Writing Facilitation Strategies

Strategies for facilitating writing are similar for either emergent literacy learners or children who demonstrate delayed development. For children exhibiting typical patterns of learning, the strategies presented will simply enhance the learning that is already occurring. For children exhibiting difficulty representing information through writing, the strategies will provide the necessary support to progress along the developmental continuum.

This chapter begins with a discussion of five general principles that underlie the use of all writing facilitation strategies. Section two provides a list and description of the specific writing facilitation strategies. Section three includes examples of the facilitation strategies in use. The chapter concludes with a list of writing goals and objectives appropriate for different developmental levels.

Principles for Facilitating Emergent Writing

Regardless of the age or developmental level of the child, there are five basic principles to consider when facilitating writing.

> ### Principles for Facilitating Emergent Writing
>
> 1. Provide a context for the child's writing.
>
> 2. Provide meaningful reasons to write.
>
> 3. Provide meaning-based feedback.
>
> 4. Allow for and accept individuality.
>
> 5. Ensure success.

1. Provide a Context

Provide a context for the child's writing. A context may be established through joint storybook reading or discussion of an action-based picture. Storybooks should be at a developmentally-appropriate level as described in Chapter 3, pages 40-41. Pictures that illustrate an event, such as children in a park trying to catch butterflies to put in a jar, are better suited for establishing a context than single-action pictures, such as a girl licking an ice cream cone. Event pictures depict a variety of relationships that the child can represent through drawing and/or writing. Avoid pictures that are extremely busy, as there is often too much information in one picture for the young child to process for writing. Both contexts, stories and pictures, should illustrate events that are meaningful to the child.

2. A Meaningful Reason to Write

Provide the child with a meaningful reason to write. Writing is a communicative act. For a writing activity to be meaningful to a child, the child must feel a need or desire to express an idea. For example, you could use this butterfly picture* in the following activity:

> While looking at the picture, conduct a discussion on the pros and cons of using a net to catch butterflies. Prompt the child to generate her own ideas about how to catch butterflies. After this interaction, she could draw and/or write a story telling how she would catch a butterfly.

Providing an audience also establishes a sincere and meaningful reason to write. For example, following the discussion about catching a butterfly, ask the child to draw a picture for Mom that shows the kind of butterfly the children in the story caught.

3. Meaning-Based Feedback

Provide the child with meaning-based feedback. Because drawing and writing are communicative acts, focus the feedback on the message depicted in the drawing or expressed through the writing. Focusing on the content of the message acknowledges the child's communicative attempt. This type of feedback also provides information that the child can use to refine or add to his or her current understanding of a concept or idea.

Feedback that focuses foremost on the form of the child's drawing or writing sends the message that the quality of the drawing or writing is more important than the message it conveys. Children who primarily receive this type of feedback often demonstrate less risk-taking behavior in their drawing and writing because they become concerned about their work being "right."

*Arwood, Ellen Lucas, Ed.D., CCC-SLP (1985). *APRICOT I.* Reprinted with permission of Apricot, Inc.; PO Box 18191; Portland, OR 97218.

4. Allow for and Accept Individuality

Allow for and accept individuality in children's drawing and writing. Young children's ability to symbolize their world through drawing and writing is variable. Some children make very detailed drawings before they are ready to write their stories. Others quickly draw their ideas and write their stories without prompting. Still others are hesitant in attempting the drawing and/or the writing. On a given day, a child who typically writes without prompting may refuse to write anything. Given the variability within and across children, select those strategies most appropriate for the child's skills being presented at that particular moment.

5. Ensure Success

Ensure success in all drawing and writing activities. Just as adults expect children to make errors in learning to speak, so should they expect children to exhibit "errors" in their writing. Learning to write is a gradual process. Children's drawing and writing attempts will be successful when adults acknowledge the communicative intent, not the quality of the writing. Continued improvement and success is fostered by providing meaning-based feedback (described in principle 3). This feedback focuses on the message first and foremost, while providing information that children may use to refine their writing.

Specific Facilitation Strategies

The following techniques, listed in the box on page 76, may be used to facilitate writing development. Some strategies will be useful for both drawing and writing; some are more specific to either mode of graphic representation. The strategies are not presented in a developmental hierarchy. The choice of strategy depends on the child's level of emergent writing. Choose a strategy appropriate for the level of writing being demonstrated at that moment in time. In addition, begin with the least-directive technique to allow the child to demonstrate his or her individual level of performance. Use more directive strategies, such as hand-over-hand or tracing, as needed to ensure success.

1. Planning Strategies

Planning strategies are used to get the child ready to write. These strategies help the child develop a focus for the writing. They also help the child clarify and organize the ideas to be written. Planning strategies help the child to develop a better understanding of the story concepts so that the drawing and writing is easier. More than one planning strategy may be used during any given interaction.

Writing Facilitation Strategies

1. Planning Strategies

    verbal rehearsal

    drawing before writing

    semantic map

    enacting the story

2. Eliciting Strategies

    hand-over-hand

    grounding

    providing a picture

    tracing

    dictation

    pretend writing

    environmental print

    known letters

    pictographs

    first letter/pretend writing combination

    invented spelling

    copying

    power writing

    verbal prompts and questions

3. Reinforcing Strategies

    picture reading

    reading the story verbatim

    storybook as spelling reference

    asking others

Verbal Rehearsal

Verbal rehearsal involves discussion of the topic prior to writing or drawing. The discussion helps the child determine the specific content and general organization of the writing. Verbal rehearsal may occur while looking at the storybook or event picture. Both the verbal rehearsal and looking at the picture may be necessary to assist the child in formulating the ideas. Verbal rehearsal is typically the first planning strategy used.

"Tell me what the first little pig did to build a house."

"What was your favorite part of the story?"

"What would you do if a wolf showed up at your door?"

"Let's look to see what the second house was made of."

Drawing Before Writing

Ask the child to draw a picture prior to writing. Drawing the picture first helps the child organize and refine the information to be included in the written story. The drawing also provides a visual representation of the child's story that the child can refer to while writing. Drawing prior to writing is particularly important because beginning writers lack automaticity in the motor aspects of writing. They often forget what they want to say while concentrating on the movement of the pencil or selection of letters for spelling words.

Semantic Map

Create a semantic map using pictures copied from the book or an event picture. Have the children select and arrange two or three pictures that tell a story. Then have the children use the semantic map as they draw or write the story.

Enacting the Story

Enact or role-play a scene from the story. Performing the physical actions of the characters helps children refine their understanding of the story events. Children are more willing and better able to write their stories when they have a clear understanding of the story events.

2. Eliciting Strategies

Eliciting strategies help the child graphically represent what he or she understands about the story.

Hand-over-Hand

Hand-over-hand provides direct assistance in helping the child begin or complete an element of the drawing or the written story. The facilitator places a hand over the child's hand so that the drawing or writing can be completed together. Use this strategy with a child who is reluctant to draw or write or when less-direct strategies do not provide enough support for the child to be successful. This strategy ensures success and serves to promote more risk-taking behavior in future writing endeavors.

Grounding

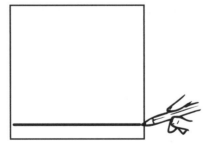

Grounding provides a concrete starting point for the child's drawing. The facilitator draws a line on the paper to represent the ground. This line provides the child a visual reference point for beginning the drawing.

Providing a Picture

Provide a picture as a reference for children to look at while drawing or writing. This strategy is particularly useful for children who are unable to begin without some visual support. However, first encourage the children to draw what they can. If necessary, show the picture and then remove it again. This strategy may not be appropriate for some children, especially those who draw every detail of the picture before writing. For children who are overly intent on duplicating the picture, consider other elicitation strategies.

Tracing

Have the child trace a picture or an object. Having successfully drawn something on the paper, the child may be coaxed into adding features or different items to the drawing. This strategy is an initial step for the child who is reluctant to draw and should be used sparingly. Encourage and support risk-taking behavior as soon as possible.

Dictation

Dictation occurs when the child tells the facilitator what to write. The facilitator writes the message using the type of writing (words, pictographs, or a combination) most appropriate to the child's level of development. Although typically used for beginning writers, dictation also may be used for children who write independently but get tired from writing before they have expressed all their ideas.

Pretend Writing

Pretend writing is a descriptive term that refers to the use of cursive-like lines to represent conventional writing. Demonstrate this writing for children who are reluctant to write, but avoid using the term *pretend writing* with children because it communicates that their attempts are not considered writing. Some children may produce pretend writing naturally; for reluctant writers, pretend writing provides a bridge to more conventional writing.

Environmental Print

Use the environment as a source for writing. Children may scan the room for letters and use any materials in sight that contain letters to assist them in their writing.

Known Letters

Encourage children to use any known letters for writing. Often children know one or two letters from their names. Initially, these letters may be used to represent the story. This strategy serves to reinforce the concept that ideas can be represented graphically and utilizes children's current writing knowledge as a starting point.

Pictographs

Write pictographs or rebus symbols above the child's pretend writing or to record the child's dictated story. Use pictographs instead of words or in combination with words. Children can suggest a picture that would best represent and help them remember a word.

Pictographs allow those children who are unable to read orthographic print to read their stories at a later time. Furthermore, pairing pictographs with words promotes reading fluency for beginning readers and helps develop word-recognition skills.

Sally rode her bike.

First Letter/Pretend Writing Combination

When children are in a transitional stage between pretend writing and invented spelling, prompt children to use a letter to represent the first sound of the word. Because the first sound is the most salient part of a word, children typically can represent that sound with a letter. Allow the children to use symbols or pretend writing to finish the word. This strategy helps children develop flow in writing before they can write independently using conventional spelling. With a reduced focus on spelling, children are less likely to forget the ideas they were trying to communicate.

Invented Spelling

Encourage children to use invented spelling. As they learn sound-letter associations, encourage children to spell words by the way they think the words look or sound.

Copying

Have the child copy a dictated story. This strategy provides the child an opportunity to see and use conventional spelling and serves as a step toward independent writing. To facilitate transfer, place the copying source on a flat surface near the child. Copying from a paper lying on a desk, table, or floor (flat surface) is easier than copying from a vertical surface, such as a chalkboard or a chart.

Power Writing

For children at the higher end of the developmental continuum, introduce the idea of power writing. Ask children to write their ideas on paper as fast as they can without worrying about spelling, punctuation, or neatness. Tell the children that they will have time later to check spelling and rewrite for neatness.

This strategy is particularly useful for children who are concerned that every word must be spelled correctly. Because they are concentrating on spelling, these children often forget what they want to say. With this strategy, introduce the concept of writing drafts in which children are given opportunities to check their spelling.

Verbal Prompts and Questions

Verbal prompts and questioning strategies assist children in refining their drawing or writing. Use general or specific statements or questions, such as binary choice or constituent questions.

> *Binary question:* Is it a girl or a boy raking the leaves?

> *Constituent question:* Who's raking the leaves?

Use these strategies judiciously and only to help the child clarify important aspects of the story for the reader, not to have the child draw or write a perfect story.

3. Reinforcing Strategies

Reinforcing strategies provide children with meaning-based feedback. These strategies also support writing by providing children opportunities to communicate the written message to others.

Picture Reading

Give meaning to the child's drawing by reading the picture even when the child cannot tell a story from what was drawn. This strategy reinforces the communicative nature of drawing. After reading the picture, the facilitator may follow-up with a strategy that provides the child with options for how to write what was just read, such as pretend writing or environmental letters. Here is an example:

> The child draws a picture of a cat. The facilitator reads the picture, "The cat is hungry for some milk. Let's put some words to go with your story." (The facilitator points to where the words should go.)

Reading the Story Verbatim

Read back what the children have written. For children at the higher end of the developmental continuum, read the story verbatim. This provides the children an opportunity to decide if the story "sounds right" or if changes are needed. Providing a sharing time for children to read their stories to peers or adults serves a similar function. Children learn about the need to revise or edit their writing when a concept is unclear to a listener.

Storybook As Spelling Reference

Have children use the storybook as a reference to check the spelling of a word. The children may use the book independently to find the target word, or the facilitator may tell the children that the target word is located on a specific page. This strategy increases children's awareness of word structure (phonological awareness) for authentic purposes.

Asking Others

Allow children to ask peers or a facilitator how to spell a word.

Examples of Facilitation Strategies

The following section provides actual samples of children's drawings and writing. Each sample is described, and examples of how to use the facilitation strategies are provided. For ease of understanding, strategies are presented separately for drawing and writing. Remember that this is an artificial division. In actual practice, strategies are implemented in an integrated manner that may simultaneously influence both drawing and writing.

Example 1: Drawing Without Writing

The first example is Daniel's drawing (Figure 1, page 84) completed after a discussion of the picture on the right.* Daniel's representation of the story included a rake, a bag for the leaves (large circle), and the leaves (small circle). He did not use any form of writing (scribbles, pretend writing, letters, or other symbols) to represent his story; however, he orally told the following story about his drawing: "She's pushing the leaves into the deal."

Drawing

Daniel's level of representation in the drawing is lacking in several respects. First, and most importantly, no agent (person or animal) who can perform an action is present, although he does refer to a girl in his oral story as he says, "She's pushing the leaves into the deal." Through this oral statement, Daniel indicates that he understands the need for a person to perform the action of raking.

Further evaluation of the drawing provides additional information about Daniel's understanding of his world. The drawing of the rake includes all the important features of the object (a handle for a person to hold on to and the tines used to gather the leaves). Additionally, he exhibits some understanding of size relative to the two objects (bag and leaves) as indicated by the large and small circles. The two circles are drawn with little detail, making the objects unrecognizable to a person unfamiliar with the original picture. However, through a verbal explanation, a child with limited drawing skills can make the marks represent a variety of objects.

*Arwood, Ellen Lucas, Ed.D., CCC-SLP (1985). *APRICOT I.* Reprinted with permission of Apricot, Inc.; PO Box 18191; Portland, OR 97218.

Daniel

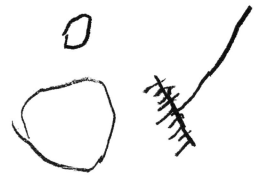

She's pushing the leaves into the deal.

Figure 1

Strategies

Because the most important element missing in this drawing is the agent, the best place to begin facilitation is with the agent.

> Facilitator: I see that the rake is lying on the ground, but there are still leaves that need to be put in the bag. Who's going to rake the leaves into the bag?
>
> (or)
>
> In the story you told me, you said that "she's" pushing the leaves into the bag, but I don't see her.

These are examples of open-ended prompts. If Daniel recognizes the need for the agent after these prompts, drawing should begin. If he does not realize that he needs to include a person to rake the leaves, then try using a more direct prompt.

> Facilitator: You need to draw the girl using the rake to put the leaves in the bag.
>
> (or)
>
> You need to draw the girl holding the rake in her hands.

Notice the difference between the last two statements. The wording *using the rake* implies, but does not directly state, that the girl should be holding the rake. The second example uses wording that is more visual and direct by saying that the girl is *holding the rake in her hands.* Following either of these prompts, Daniel should be provided an opportunity to add the agent to the drawing. If Daniel is still unable to draw the agent, it may be because he does not know what to draw, or he does not know where or how to draw a person.

> Facilitator: Let's look at the picture and see who was raking the leaves. See, this girl is holding the rake in her hands, and she's gathering the leaves into a pile. You need to draw a girl raking your leaves.

Provide an opportunity for Daniel to draw the girl. It is acceptable for him to look at the picture as he draws his own girl. If he does not begin drawing, you may point to where he should draw the girl. If this still is not sufficient information,

continued on next page

draw a line to represent the ground. Additional assistance may be supplied by verbally walking Daniel through the drawing process, with or without using a hand-over-hand technique.

> Facilitator: Okay, Daniel, here is the ground. What part of a person's body touches the ground? That's right, her feet are on the ground. Let's look at the picture to see what her feet are connected to.

This procedure continues until the basic parts of the girl are represented on paper. Remember that the goal is to help Daniel represent his ideas symbolically on paper, not to help him draw a perfect picture.

A review of Daniel's drawing reveals other areas that could be refined using a variety of strategies. For example, Daniel drew one leaf, but his oral story indicated that the girl was pushing *leaves* into the bag. You could bring this discrepancy to the child's attention through a number of statements, such as the following:

> Facilitator: You told me that the girl is pushing the leaves into the bag, but I only see one leaf (as you point to the single small circle).

If the child does not respond to this open-ended prompt, follow-up with a more specific statement or question:

> Facilitator: Where are the other leaves she needs to rake into the bag?
>
> (or)
>
> Did she already rake all the leaves except that one into the bag?

Exercise your own judgment regarding the number of elements in the drawing to address in one session. Remember that the idea is not to attain a perfect drawing but to assist the child in a better understanding of his world.

Writing

Although Daniel told a story about his drawing, he did not attempt to represent his oral story using written symbols, such as scribbles, pretend writing, or letters.

Strategies

The facilitator should encourage Daniel to "write the story" after he has completed his drawing.

> Facilitator: Now that you have drawn your story, I would like you to write your story.
>
> (or)
>
> You read your story for me, but I don't see where the words are.

If Daniel is reluctant to write or says that he doesn't know how, remind him that he can write using any letters he knows or letters he sees around the room.

You could also demonstrate pretend writing. Children sometimes say they can't read their own pretend writing. If that happens, assure the child that he will be able to read the writing because he wrote it. Remind him to look at his picture if he forgets what he wrote.

Example 2: Drawing with Pretend Writing

The next illustration (Figure 2, page 88) is a depiction of the same picture as Figure 1 approximately two weeks later. In terms of content, this drawing included an agent (Jennifer holding onto the rake) and a pile of leaves. Note that the drawing of the agent included the most relevant parts: the body, arms, legs, head, eyes, and mouth. Although hands were not depicted, the rake handle is in an appropriate relationship with the arm to give the impression that Jennifer is holding onto the rake. The relationship of the rake to the leaves also indicates a clear understanding of what Jennifer is doing with the rake. Daniel's oral telling of his drawing included all the pictured ideas: "Jennifer is raking the leaves into a pile."

Figure 2

Drawing

Daniel's drawing reflects a significant improvement over the course of two weeks. Facilitation during that time period included discussion of the same picture to allow for concept refinement through repeated exposure. This refinement is reflected in Daniel's drawing, primarily in the inclusion of a well-developed agent. Other notable improvement in this drawing is the addition of more leaves to match the plural marker in his oral story.

Strategy

The most powerful strategy for facilitating improved drawing in this example was the facilitator's use of repeated exposure. Given the improved quality of Daniel's drawing in a short period of time, no further strategies for addressing drawing are suggested for this example. Use repeated reading or discussion for both storybooks and event pictures.

Writing

The most apparent writing difference is the inclusion of pretend writing that extends down both the left and right sides of the paper. In the previous drawing, no writing was included. Although there is a mismatch between the quantity of Daniel's pretend writing and the quantity of words used to express his story, this mismatch is not a concern at this point in time. A first step, discussed in the previous strategy section, was for Daniel to understand that the stories he depicts through drawing may also be expressed through writing. He demonstrated understanding of the drawing-writing connection in this sample. With time, Daniel can be shown how the written symbols are segmented into words with each group of symbols representing one word.

Strategies

Writing facilitation should focus on strengthening Daniel's understanding that writing is another means to symbolize ideas.

Facilitator: I see you wrote your story. Please read it to me.

The facilitator should demonstrate for Daniel how to read by moving his finger along the pretend writing, beginning from the left and moving to the right.

Example 3: Drawing with Segmented Pretend Writing

This next sample (Figure 3a, page 91) was produced after discussion of the book *The Blueberry Bears* (Lapp, 1983). This story traces the exploits of a group of bears as they break in and rummage through Bessie's cabin, eating all the blueberries they can find. The drawing depicts two views: the outside of the house to show where the action took place and the refrigerator that held the only blueberries the bears couldn't find. The pretend writing is segmented with each word represented by a separate and distinct squiggle. When reading her story, Heather pointed to each individual squiggle as she said the words. Heather also independently wrote her name on her drawing.

Drawing

In this example, Heather's drawing consists of two important elements of the story, but her drawing is different from the previous examples. In the previous two examples, the children's written words described what was happening in the drawings. In this example, the picture no longer tells the entire story. Rather, the drawing is functioning to set the scene, and the written words go beyond describing the drawing.

Writing

Heather's writing (separate and distinct squiggles) illustrates a clear understanding of wordness. Compare this writing with the sample completed three months earlier (Figure 3b, page 92). In Figure 3b, Heather used undifferentiated pretend writing with a mismatch between the amount of writing she produced and the length of her oral story. In the current sample, the pretend writing is segmented, and the amount of writing matches the length of the verbal story.

Strategies

Note the facilitator's writing above Heather's pretend writing. Printing the words above the child's writing serves several purposes. First, it acknowledges to the child that the facilitator was listening. Second, the printed words provide a model for Heather to use in future writing. Finally, many of the words Heather used in her oral story were words used in the book. Printing the words again provides another exposure to the same words. This redundancy helps to build a sight-word vocabulary in a natural and meaningful manner.

continued next page

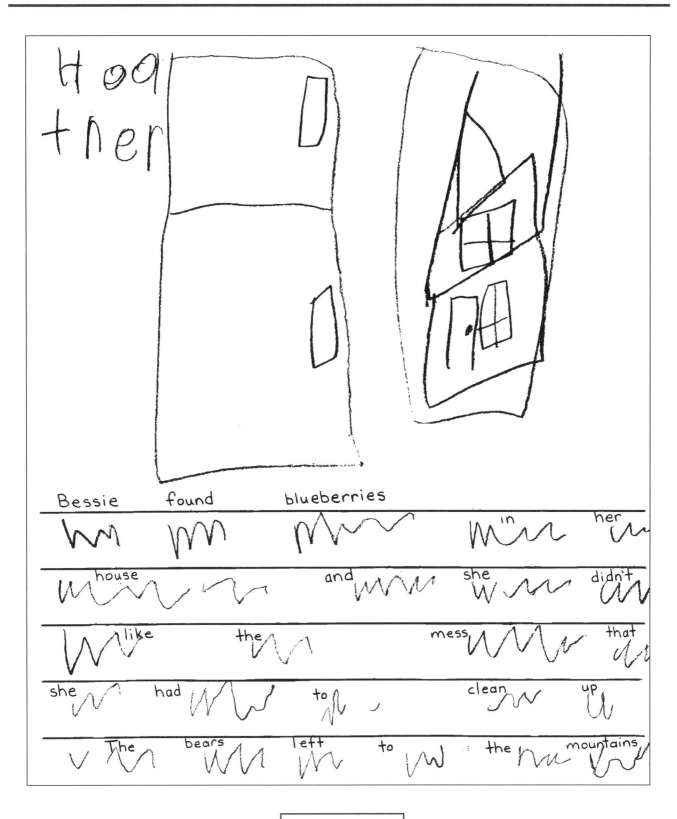

Figure 3a

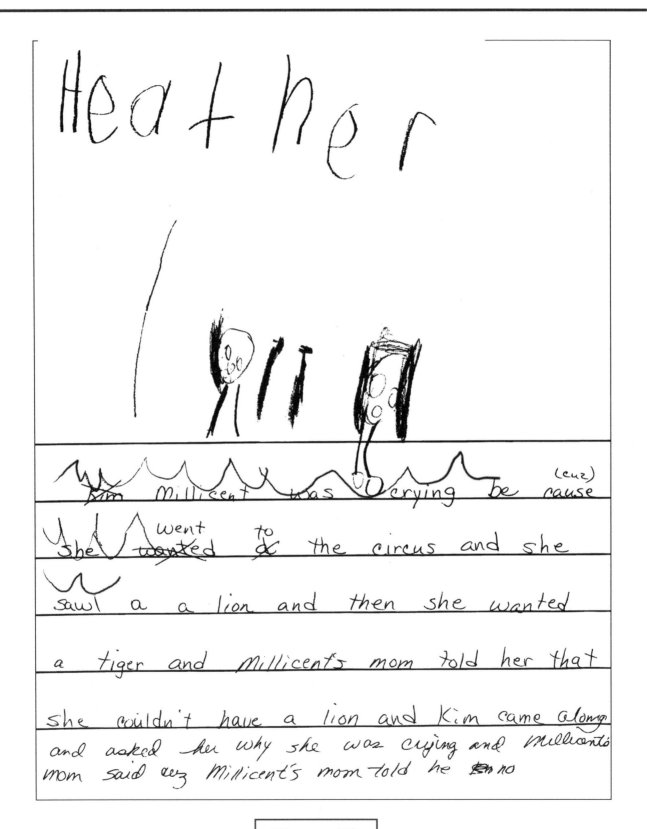

Heather

~~Kim~~ Millicent was crying be cause (cuz)

She ~~wanted~~ went to the circus and she

sawl a a lion and then she wanted

a tiger and millicents mom told her that

she couldn't have a lion and Kim came along
and asked her why she was crying and Millicents
mom said cuz Millicent's mom told he ~~an~~ no

Figure 3b

After children begin to write their stories but before they use letter combinations to represent words, facilitation should reinforce the communicative purpose of writing. Verbal responses to the drawing or to the oral story should always focus on the meaning being conveyed.

Facilitator: (responding to the last idea of Heather's story) Yes, the bears have left Bessie's house. (Point to the picture to acknowledge that the bears are nowhere to be seen.)

(responding to the idea about having cleaned up the house) Bessie did a good job cleaning up after the bears. There aren't any blueberry smudges left on the refrigerator.

Both Heather's printing of her name and her pretend writing suggest that she understands left-to-right progression. Although she wrote her name on two lines, the *t* was written at the left edge of the paper. Splitting a word when there is no more space is common in young children's writing. They may also continue writing down the right edge of the paper or anywhere there is space. The following strategy may serve to heighten the child's awareness of standard conventions for organizing writing:

Facilitator: I see that you started to write your name but did not finish it. (Point to the letter *a* and slide your finger to the right where the rest of her name should be printed. Pause to allow the child to respond.)

(If the child says or points to the letters *ther* on the second line, explain that a reader expects all of a name to be written on the same line. If the child does not indicate that the remaining letters are on the next line, cue the child.)

Facilitator: I see some letters here. It says *ther* (rhymes with *were*). I'm not sure what that means.

(If the child does not respond that those letters are part of her name, say the following:)

You need to write your name with all the letters on the same line. (Provide a model of how her name would look.)

Example 4: Drawing with Letters and Pretend Writing

Figure 4 (page 95) represents Sara's interpretation of the same story event from *The Blueberry Bears*. Her drawing shows Bessie with her mop, cleaning up after the bears. The two figures to the left represent her dog (the larger figure) and cat (the smaller figure). The opened freezer displays the only remaining blueberries (small circles), and the square marked with an *X* symbolizes the refrigerator. Sara's written story includes a mixture of words spelled solely with letters and words spelled with a beginning letter and pretend writing.

Drawing

Unlike the previous sample, Sara's drawing of the event not only establishes the setting, but also includes the character's action. Her rendition of Bessie includes the necessary body parts, even fingers with which to grasp the mop. The animals, though, are not clearly differentiated from each other.

Strategies

Although the story ideas are depicted well, facilitation strategies could be used to help refine Sara's representation of the animals.

Facilitator: I know that Bessie had two pets, a cat and a dog, but I cannot really tell in your drawing which one is the dog and which one is the cat. Can you think of one thing that makes a cat look different from a dog?

Provide Sara with an opportunity to generate a distinctive feature for one of the animals and then add it to her drawing. If she is unable to think of a difference, refer to the book for a visual comparison of the two animals.

Facilitator: Let's look in the book to see how dogs and cats are different.

Sara is provided with an opportunity to pick out a feature difference and draw it. If she still needs assistance, the facilitator can select a feature.

Facilitator: Look at the difference between the ears. A dog's ears are longer and bigger than a cat's ears.

Figure 4

Writing

Sara's written story demonstrates an understanding of the writing process. Notice that each word is represented with an appropriate letter matching the beginning sound of the word, such as *B* for *blue* and *H* for *hard*. Beginning sounds are often the first sounds to be represented by letters because they are more salient (easier to hear and discriminate) than middle or ending sounds. You may have noticed that the *B* on the second line does not match the word *mess* that Sara read. This error may have resulted from Sara initially formulating her written story to say "Bessie cleaned up the blueberry bears' mess and she worked hard," but when reading the story, she omitted the word *bears*. High-frequency words that Sara has encountered often in reading, such as *and* and *the*, are written in their entirety.

This sample provides an excellent example of writing that results from facilitation strategies that focus on the content of the message, not the form. Sara uses a variety of symbols to express her idea. If she knows the entire word, she writes it. If she only knows the first sound, she represents that sound and marks the remainder of the word with pretend writing. In other words, she uses all the tools in her repertoire of skills and doesn't quit if she can't spell an entire word. Sara's willingness to take risks in her writing occurred because the facilitator consistently accepted her current skills and encouraged her use of higher-level skills while focusing on the message (Principles for Facilitating Emergent Writing 3, 4, and 5).

Sara's use of capital letters within the body of the sentence should be accepted in their current form. Focusing on the mechanics of writing in the early stages of writing development often results in children being afraid to take risks and experiment with writing. As discussed earlier, printing above the child's writing serves as a scaffold or model for future writing.

Strategies

Because Sara is demonstrating a solid, beginning understanding of sound/symbol associations, the facilitator may want to provide her with additional opportunities to see and spell the words used in her story. Sara is not yet ready for spelling some of the less familiar words independently, so the facilitator could write the conventional spelling on a separate sheet of paper and have Sara copy the story. The most important focus of the activity should be creating a meaningful story, not spelling words correctly.

continued on next page

Facilitator: You wrote an interesting story about Bessie cleaning up the mess. I know you will want to take this home for your mom to read, but I would like to hang your story on our author board. Would you please write your story on this piece of paper for the author board?

Some children ask to rewrite their stories using conventional spelling. For these children, simply provide the paper and the opportunity.

Example 5: Drawing with Orthographic Writing

The final sample (Figure 5, page 98) also was produced following a discussion of *The Blueberry Bears*. This sample includes a picture of Bessie mopping up the dirty floor while checking to see if the bears found the blueberries she had stored in the freezer. Careful examination of the picture shows Bessie with a smile on her face because there are still blueberries in the bowl in the freezer (note the small dots representing the blueberries). Joe's written story, a combination of orthographic writing and dictated writing, fully describes the picture.

Drawing

At this level of development, Joe quickly drew the picture prior to writing. The drawing encompasses all the elements he wanted to include in the writing, including the detail of how Bessie felt about finding the remaining blueberries. Since all the essential elements are present in the drawing, no facilitation strategies for drawing are suggested.

Writing

In this sample, Joe's written story illustrates spelling at several different levels, including phonetic, transitional, and conventional. Words written at the phonetic level include letters representing all the phonemes of the word, but the spelling is unconventional (e.g., *opend* for *opened*; *firezir* for *freezer*).

Joe also demonstrated spelling at the transitional stage. This type of spelling goes beyond how the word sounds to incorporate orthographic principles specific to English. For example, Joe spelled the word *was* as *wus*. The use of the *S* instead of the *Z* reveals knowledge that there

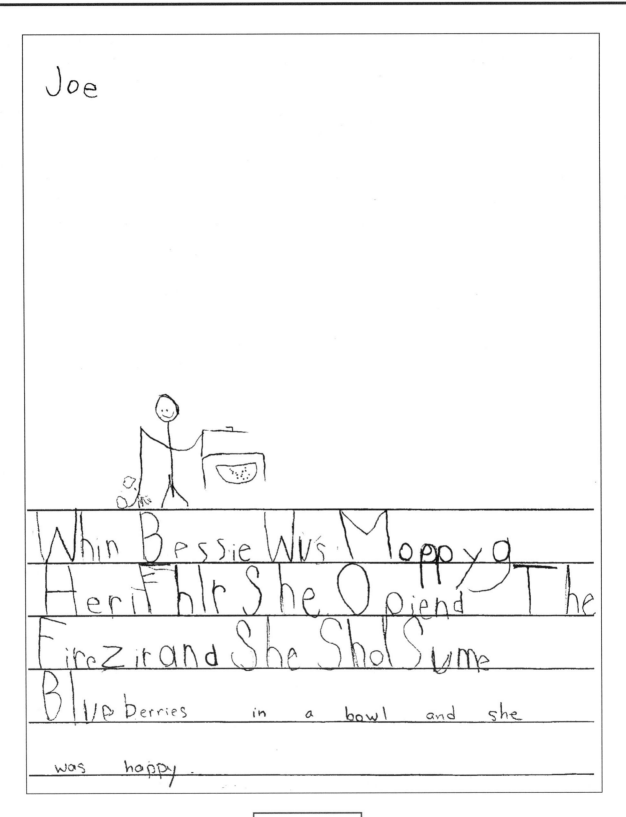

Joe

Whin Bessie Wus Moppya Heri Fhlr She Opiend The Firezir and She Shol Sume Blue berries   in   a   bowl   and   she was   happy.

Figure 5

is not always a one-to-one match between the letters used to spell a word and how a word sounds. Notice also the spelling of *some*. Although the vowel is incorrect (*sume*), Joe demonstrates knowledge of the silent -*e* rule.

Finally, conventional spelling is present in the sample. Joe spelled familiar, high frequency words such as *and, she*, and *the* using correct orthography.

Strategies

For a child who demonstrates this overall level of spelling, focus first on reacting to the meaning of the written story. Later, feedback can focus on the spelling. If the child reads the story to the facilitator, the response may be something like the following:

> Facilitator: (pointing to Bessie's smile) I can see that Bessie really is happy that the bears left her some blueberries.

After providing this feedback, the facilitator should address the spelling error(s) that have the most negative impact on the message. For this sample, the spelling of the word *floor (fhlr)* or *saw (shol)* may be most detrimental to understanding the story. Once the choice has been made, the facilitator should read that portion of the story exactly as it is written.

> Facilitator: When Bessie was mopping her fhlr . . . (with *fhlr* being read without any vowel sound except the vocalic /r/)

Several things may occur at this point. The child may assist the reader and say "floor." The facilitator responds as follows:

> Facilitator: As a reader, that is not how I expect the word *floor* to look. Can you think of any other way to spell the word so that my mouth and lips know they need to be rounded for the middle part of the word *floor*?

The *or* part of the word *floor* is exaggerated slightly to highlight the part that needs to change. The child should be watching your mouth at this time so that the visual aspects of *or* (the lip rounding and slightly open mouth) are readily apparent. Then ask the child to write the word again. (Use a separate or scratch sheet of paper to maintain the integrity of the original story.)

continued on next page

Once the child has tried the word again, provide additional feedback as necessary. The focus always remains on the reader's perception of how words should look and what the letters tell the reader's mouth to do. This technique allows the integration of the visual information provided by written letters with the motor movements (tactile-kinesthetic cues) from producing the sounds. In this example, the inclusion of the letter *O* tells the reader to open her mouth and round her lips.

Note that the last two lines include words written by the facilitator. This assistance may have resulted because of time constraints, or the child may have gotten tired. By the time the facilitator started writing, the child had already produced a significant amount of writing. Remember that writing is a complex task, so young writers get tired. It is acceptable to have a mixture of the child's own writing and dictated writing because the goal is to reinforce the concept of writing as a means of communicating a message, not just a task to be finished.

Writing Goals and Objectives

Drawing

Goal: The child will draw topic-related pictures demonstrating improved organization of ideas and relationships between people, objects, and actions depicted.

Objectives: The child will:

- Draw a picture related to the topic or story.

- Draw a picture with an agent present.

- Draw a picture with all parts of an agent present.

- Draw a picture with parts in proper spatial position and orientation.

- Draw a picture from stick figures to thick or proportional figures (three dimensional).

- Draw a picture including all elements appropriate to the event (illustrating actions of characters and objects).

- Draw a picture representing emotions of characters.

- Draw a picture minimizing unnecessary elements.

Writing Conventions

Goal: The child will develop the basic conventions of writing.

Objectives: The child will:

- Write about a picture he or she has drawn.

- Use pretend writing to represent pictured ideas.

- Use pretend writing with spacing that represents words.

- Write from top to bottom of the paper.

- Write from left to right on the paper.

- Write using letters.

- Write using the first sounds of words.

- Write using spaces between letter combinations to represent words.

- Increase the number of words spelled correctly.

Writing Content

Goal: The child will increase the complexity of topic-related ideas represented in writing.

Objectives: The child will:

- Label a person or setting.

- Describe an action, an event, or a person.

- Interpret an action or an event.

- Increase the number of topic-related ideas written.

- Increase the number of words written about the topic.

- Increase the number of complete versus incomplete ideas.

Engaging children in meaningful interactions with print enhances their early literacy development. This chapter provides a guide for planning literacy activities using storybooks and event pictures. The activities are intended to incorporate the general principles for facilitating reading and writing described in Chapters 3 and 5. These activities are appropriate for use in individual and group settings and are easily adapted to any child's developmental level.

Facilitated Reading

Procedure for Facilitating Reading

1. Select appropriate materials.

2. Divide the story into event segments.

3. Determine the focus of the story.

4. Assemble props.

5. Conduct facilitated reading.

1. Select appropriate materials.

The first step in reading is to select a book or an event picture appropriate to the child's developmental level. A list of suggested books is provided in Chapter 8, pages 142-144. Selection of appropriate books and materials also is discussed in Chapter 3 in "General Principles for Facilitating Emergent Reading," pages 30-41.

2. Divide the story into event segments.

Divide the story (book or event picture) into segments that allow for discussion and elaboration of one or two events. Limiting the number of pages read or the number of ideas discussed about a story serves the following functions:

- Allows time to fully discuss and develop the implicit and explicit meanings and relationships expressed in the pictures and words

- Allows the child to actively participate in story construction

- Allows the facilitator to discover what the child already knows

Much of the information in pictures and print is implied. For example, in the *Mrs. Wishy-washy* story, Mrs. Wishy-washy is standing with her hands on her hips (see page 107). Adult facilitators automatically recognize the implied meaning of Mrs. Wishy-washy's behavior: she is upset. Young children may need to have those implicit meanings made explicit. Developing those explicit meanings takes time.

To understand implicit and explicit information and to ensure the child's full participation, facilitators should co-construct the story. This active participation is necessary for the child to assimilate new information. For example, in *Mrs. Wishy-washy,* allow time for the child to touch the cow in the book or to act like the cow jumping into a mud puddle. Through co-construction, the facilitator discovers what the child knows and what additional information is needed.

3. Determine the focus of the story.

Select concepts to develop for each new event segment. These focal points should be those elements critical to the story's meaning, including characters, their actions, or implied or explicit information. Predetermining a story focus will provide ideas for presenting the information. Consider the child's responses, and incorporate those ideas into the story construction.

4. Assemble props.

For children at the early developmental levels of reading, use props to increase understanding and participation in story construction. For example, when reading *Mrs. Wishy-washy,* a child could use a miniature cow to jump in the puddle on the storybook page.

5. Conduct facilitated reading.

Facilitated reading involves using the reading strategies presented in previous chapters in this book. The first reading of each predetermined segment establishes general information about the story, such as the characters and events. With each successive reading, review old segments and introduce a new segment. This repeated reading is critical for increasing the child's level of participation in the story-construction process.

Facilitators often find it difficult to review previously-read segments at increasing levels of language complexity. The chart on page 105 provides a framework for conducting repeated readings. Although the goals listed in the chart are presented in a hierarchy, more than one goal can be incorporated into a single session, depending on the child's needs.

Goals for Repeated Readings

Reading 1

Goal: Establish the relationships on the page.

- Use facilitating strategies to identify the people, objects, and actions.

Reading 2

Goal: Re-establish and solidify information from the previous reading.

- Have the child retell elements of the story.

- Increase the use of open-ended questions to determine what the child knows about the story and what information needs to be clarified.

- End each page with a summary of the event represented in the picture.

Reading 3

Goal: Expand the information that was established in the two previous readings by including more detail and going beyond the pictures and the text.

- Develop unfamiliar vocabulary.

- Include personal experiences.

- Ask more semantically-complex questions that include motives, causes, interpretations of feelings, or predictions.

continued on next page

Reading 4

Goal: Develop print awareness by directing the child's attention to the printed text.

- Point out words or letters on the page.

- Find the letter that begins the child's name.

- Count the number of words on a page or letters in a word.

- Discuss long versus short words.

- Encourage the child to read the page aloud.

Facilitated Writing

Procedure for Facilitating Writing

1. Determine the focus of the story.

2. Develop a meaningful activity.

3. Assemble materials.

5. Conduct facilitated writing.

1. Determine the focus of the story.

As with facilitated reading, the story focus for writing needs to be established first. Since writing immediately follows each reading session, the writing activity should be an elaboration of the ideas developed in the story.

2. Develop a meaningful activity.

Determine a meaningful reason for writing in conjunction with selecting the story focus. The writing activity must be meaningful from the child's point of view and should be a means of communicating rather than just a task to be completed. Therefore, the facilitator needs to create a reason for writing or drawing.

3. Assemble materials.

Provide a variety of writing materials and tools. This collection may include paper of different sizes, colors, and textures, with and without lines. Choices in writing tools may include pencils, pens, crayons, markers, paints, etc. This variety allows for creativity and personal expression in writing.

4. Conduct facilitated writing.

Each writing session immediately follows the facilitated reading. Writing will focus on a topic related to the reading. Typically, each writing activity will be completed in a single session.

Literacy Units

The following literacy units are developed around a book or event picture. The first unit includes an expanded example using facilitated reading and writing with a group of children during four readings of the book.

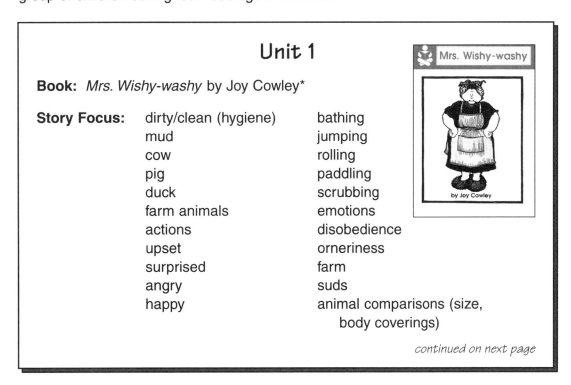

Unit 1

Book: *Mrs. Wishy-washy* by Joy Cowley*

Story Focus:	dirty/clean (hygiene)	bathing
	mud	jumping
	cow	rolling
	pig	paddling
	duck	scrubbing
	farm animals	emotions
	actions	disobedience
	upset	orneriness
	surprised	farm
	angry	suds
	happy	animal comparisons (size, body coverings)

continued on next page

* Cowley, J. (1990). *Mrs. Wishy-washy.* Reprinted with the permission of The Wright Group, 19201 120th Avenue NE, Bothell, WA 98011, 1-800-523-2371.

Writing Suggestions

Draw: a picture of your favorite animal.

what you think the brush and soap are for.

how the animals looked when they got in the mud.

other ways animals get dirty.

what Mrs. Wishy-washy did when she saw the dirty animals.

how you would clean the animals.

where the animals live.

something else Mrs. Wishy-washy could wash.

yourself doing something you enjoy.

why the animals got in the mud.

Mrs. Wishy-washy's expression after she finished washing the animals.

Extension Activities

Extension activities are provided to demonstrate how to include literacy in different types of activities, such as snack time, music, art, and dramatic play. Throughout these activities, reinforce the concepts developed in the story. These suggestions may be particularly helpful for professionals who work with the same children for extended periods of time, such as half-day or all-day preschool centers.

Music: "Old MacDonald Had a Farm"

"Bingo"

"Five Little Ducks"

"Mud" (tune: "Mary Had a Little Lamb")

"This Is the Way We Wash" (tune: "The Mulberry Bush")

Mud

Mud is very nice to feel,
Nice to feel, nice to feel.
Mud is very nice to feel,
All squishy between the toes!

I'd rather wade in wiggly mud,
Wiggly mud, wiggly mud.
I'd rather wade in wiggly mud,
Than smell a yellow rose.

continued on next page

This Is the Way We Wash

This is the way we wash the cow,
Wash the cow, wash the cow.
This is the way we wash the cow,
So early in the morning.

Verse 2: pig

Verse 3: duck

Verse 4: anything the children choose that can be washed

Snacks: pigs in a blanket
animal crackers dipped in chocolate pudding or melted chocolate
pancakes in the shapes of animals
cheese sandwiches cut out with animal-shaped cookie cutters

Involve the children in all aspects of snack time, including planning, preparation, and cleanup.

Pigs in a Blanket

12 cocktail franks
6 ready-to-bake crescent rolls

Remove six crescent rolls from the tube, and cut each in half. Wrap one-half of a crescent roll around each cocktail frank. Place them on a cookie sheet, and bake at 375 degrees for 15 minutes.

Animal Pancakes

This activity combines art and snack time. Children draw pictures of the animals they want for their pancakes. Prepare pancake mix according to directions on the box. Use the children's pictures to make an animal pancake for each child.

Dramatic Play: Children take turns role-playing the characters in the story. *Mrs. Wishy-washy* is a good story to act out because the actions are familiar and the dialogue is simple and repetitive.

continued on next page

Children make props for washing clothes. Use discarded cardboard boxes to create a washer and dryer. These items may be used when role-playing the story or placed in a housekeeping area for children to incorporate into their play throughout the day.

Other Activities:

Muddy Footprints

Make mud with the children by mixing dirt and water. Allow children to add different amounts of water to experience varying consistencies of mud. Spread out butcher paper and let children walk across the paper, making muddy footprints. When they get to the end of the paper, have the children wash their feet in soapy water. Finger paints also work well to do this activity.

Charting

For children at more advanced levels, the facilitator can assist in charting the similarities and differences among the animals. Compare physical features, such as size, body covering (hair, feathers), number of legs, type of feet, and different kinds of ears and tails. Use words and pictures to fill in the chart.

On pages 111-114, there is an example of implementing Unit 1 to facilitate reading and writing. The full unit would involve seven sessions of reading and rereading the story. The first four sessions are illustrated here for your reference.

Unit 1: Expanded Example

Reading 1: Cover, title page, pages 2 and 3
Reading 2: Cover through page 5
Reading 3: Cover through page 7
Reading 4: Cover through page 11
Reading 5: Cover through page 13
Reading 6: Cover through page 16
Reading 7: Entire book

Reading 1

Story Focus: farm animals, mud, cleaning, clothing, emotions, jumping

Prop: miniature cow

Hold the book up and show the children the cover.* Ask an open-ended question.

> Facilitator: What do you see?
>
> (or)
>
> Who do you think this is?

Let the children share what they know; any answer is acceptable. (Be sure to establish Mrs. Wishy-washy's name.)

Draw attention to unfamiliar objects that the children do not mention. For example, point to the apron and say:

> Facilitator: Oh, look, she's wearing an apron. (Pause for children to comment.) And she has her hair pulled up in a ____.

Remember that the children should be co-constructing the story, so active participation is a must. For some children, pointing and using gestures may be as appropriate as verbal responses. For example, following the cloze procedure, hold the book out so the children can touch the scarf.

continued on next page

---

* Cowley, J. (1990). *Mrs. Wishy-washy*. Reprinted with the permission of The Wright Group, 19201 120th Avenue NE, Bothell, WA 98011, 1-800-523-2371.

Proceed to the title page.* Direct the children's attention to the scrub brush and soap by pointing and saying:

> Facilitator: Look at these!

Pause to see if the children offer any information about the items. If they do not respond, say:

> Facilitator: I see a scrub brush and some soap.
> I wonder what these are for.

Stay with the discussion as long as children show interest in the topic. Then fold the book back so that only page 2* is showing.

> Facilitator: Oh, look, there's a _____.

(For developmentally advanced children, a verbal prompt may be sufficient. For younger children, a point may be needed.)

Wait for the children to fill in the blank. After identifying the animal as a cow, talk about the features that distinguish it from other animals, such as asking what sound a cow makes.

Show the children page 3* and say:

> Facilitator: Oh, look what the cow did!
> (Wait for children to comment.)

If children do not respond, say:

> Facilitator: (point to the cow) She _____.

This is a good time to allow the children to act out the cow's actions.

During group facilitated reading, allow all children to respond at the same time. Many behavior problems are prevented by keeping all of the children actively involved.

continued on next page

* Cowley, J. (1990). *Mrs. Wishy-washy*. Reprinted with the permission of The Wright Group, 19201 120th Avenue NE, Bothell, WA 98011, 1-800-523-2371.

Reading 2

Story Focus: farm animals, mud, dirty, rolling, emotions

Props: miniature cow and pig

Begin the session by reviewing the story read thus far. Show the children the book during the review.

> Facilitator: What was this lady's name? (Point to Mrs. Wishy-washy.)
>
> Remember what happened in the story? (Pause.)
>
> What animal did we read about? (Pause.)
>
> Tell me what the cow said. (Pause.)
>
> Did our cow say *moo*? (Pause.)

Always pause after a prompt to give children time to participate. Following a child's comment, repeat or elaborate on what the child said. Refer back to the feedback strategies in Chapter 3, pages 35-36, for additional guidance.

Discussion about the pig* should use questions similar to those used to talk about the cow.

Reading 3

Story Focus: farm animals, mud, dirty, paddling, actions, size

Props: miniature cow, pig, and duck

"Oh, lovely mud," said the pig,

and he rolled in it.

The review portion of this session involves even more elaboration about the story events already discussed. More abstract or unfamiliar concepts may be developed, such as the word *lovely* or the size of the animals.

> Facilitator: Which animal is bigger, the cow or the pig?

The review can be approached from different perspectives. For example, relate personal experiences to the story events.

continued on next page

* Cowley, J. (1990). *Mrs. Wishy-washy*. Reprinted with the permission of The Wright Group, 19201 120th Avenue NE, Bothell, WA 98011, 1-800-523-2371.

Facilitator: Have you ever gotten muddy? What happened?

(or)

Have you ever been to a farm? Tell me about it.

The topic focused on and the amount of elaboration provided depend on the children's understanding of and interests in the story events. A child's interest should not be confused with a child's ability to attend. Lack of attention may be a result of insufficient background information and/or experience with the topic. Lack of attention also may occur if the story is presented at developmentally inappropriate levels, either too high or too low. Use the children's behaviors as a cue to adjust the facilitation.

New information about the duck* should follow a format similar to the one used to discuss the cow and pig.

"Oh, lovely mud," said the duck,

and she paddled in it.

Reading 4

Story Focus: muddy, clean, bathe, surprise, scrubbing, suds

Props: miniature cow, pig, and duck; brush

This reading may involve a more direct focus on print. Turn to the cover; point to the *M* in Mrs. Wishy-washy's name, and say:

Facilitator: Mrs. Wishy-washy's name starts with the letter _____.

(or)

Whose name starts with an *M*?

(or)

Show me a letter in your name.

On a page with printed text, say:

Facilitator: Show me where to start reading. Read the words with me. (Point to each word as your read it.)

Continue these procedures through readings 5, 6, and 7.

continued on next page

* Cowley, J. (1990). *Mrs. Wishy-washy*. Reprinted with the permission of The Wright Group, 19201 120th Avenue NE, Bothell, WA 98011, 1-800-523-2371.

Writing 1

Story Focus: farm animals

Materials: paper, pencils

Facilitated Drawing: Show the picture of Mrs. Wishy-washy's cow*, and say:

"Oh, lovely mud," said the cow,

> Facilitator: Mrs. Wishy-washy has a cow on her farm. If you had a farm, what kind of animal would you have?

The discussion before drawing depends on the needs of the children. Discussion may be similar to the following:

> Facilitator: You might want a cow like Mrs. Wishy-washy's, or you might want a different animal. (Pause for children to offer ideas.) What are some other animals you might see on a farm?

If the children have little or no knowledge of farm animals, provide pictures of different animals to generate ideas for the drawings.

Most of the drawing is completed individually. When looking at each child's drawing, attend to the message being communicated. As needed, use facilitation strategies to help the child refine the drawing. Only ask for a limited number of changes (if any) and only those that affect the meaning communicated through the picture.

Facilitated Writing: Once the drawings are completed, encourage the children to write about their drawings. (Refer back to Chapter 5, pages 78-80, for options to represent writing.) To facilitate writing, say:

> Facilitator: I see you drew a cow. Tell me the name of your cow. (Pause for a response.) I'll write it on your picture. (Child dictates, facilitator writes.)
>
> (or)
>
> Let's write the name of your cow on the paper so we don't forget it. (Use hand-over-hand to assist the child.)

continued on next page

* Cowley, J. (1990). *Mrs. Wishy-washy*. Reprinted with the permission of The Wright Group, 19201 120th Avenue NE, Bothell, WA 98011, 1-800-523-2371.

(or)

Write the name of your cow on your paper so we know your cow's name.

Child: (may use pretend writing, letters, or other symbols)

Children at more advanced levels of writing development may be ready to write a simple story about their drawings. Use open-ended prompts.

Facilitator: Tell me about your picture.

(or)

Write a story about your picture.

Have the children show and read their completed stories to each other.

Writing 2

Story Focus: clean and dirty

Materials: paper, pencil, colors or markers

Facilitated Drawing: Show the children the picture of Mrs. Wishy-washy's cow and pig when they were clean,* and say:

"Oh, lovely mud," said the cow,

"Oh, lovely mud," said the pig.

Facilitator: Mrs. Wishy-washy's cow and pig were nice and clean. Now look at them. They are all ____.

and she jumped in it.

and he rolled in it.

Discuss how the animals got dirty. Then say:

Facilitator: Mrs. Wishy-washy didn't see her animals get dirty. Draw a picture to show her what happened to the cow and pig.

Have the children draw how the animals got dirty.

continued on next page

* Cowley, J. (1990). *Mrs. Wishy-washy*. Reprinted with the permission of The Wright Group, 19201 120th Avenue NE, Bothell, WA 98011, 1-800-523-2371.

Facilitated Writing: Once the drawings are completed, encourage the children to write about their drawings. To facilitate writing, say:

Facilitator: I see you drew a dirty pig. Write how he got dirty.

If the child is unable to spell the words, suggest using pretend writing or any letters that he or she knows. The child then reads the story aloud. Using conventional orthography, write the words above the child's writing.

Continue these procedures for writings 3 through 7.

Unit 2

Book: *I Just Forgot* by Mercer Mayer

Story Focus:

brushing teeth	going to school
making a mess	getting into trouble
cleaning up	puddles
chores	taking a bath
forgetting	going to bed
remembering	Mom being mad
wanting to please	right and wrong
obedience	types of clothing
family roles and responsibilities	

Writing Suggestions

Draw: what the kitchen looked like when Critter forgot to turn off the water.
how Mom and Critter will clean up the mess.
yourself or Critter brushing teeth.
what your room looks like.
what Little Critter's room should look like.
your favorite part of the story.
what will happen next in the story.
how you think the story will end.
about a time you made a mess.
yourself doing a chore.

continued on next page

Extension Activities

Music: "This Is the Way We Do Our Chores" (tune: "The Mulberry Bush")
"Rain, Rain, Go Away"
"The Wheels on the Bus"
"Everything Grows" (Raffi, 1987)

This Is the Way We Do Our Chores

Review the book and generate a list of Little Critter's chores. Copy the pictures of the jobs, or have children draw the jobs. Then use the pictures to select a job for each verse. Here are some possible verses:

. . . brush our teeth

. . . make our bed

. . . feed the dog

. . . water the plant

Snacks: hot or cold cereal
cookies and milk
lunch-box snack, such as sandwiches and fruit

Lunch-box Snack

Children list foods that they would like in their lunch boxes. Once the lists are made, children check the pantry for the listed items. If the snack is to be prepared that day, the children collect the items on the list and take them to the preparation area. The facilitator and the children fill the lunch boxes with snacks made from the available items.

The children's lists may also be used as a grocery list. The children check the pantry for items on their list and mark the items they find. The unmarked items become the grocery list. After shopping, the children unpack the groceries and check to see that all items have been purchased.

The general theme for this activity should focus on remembering to complete jobs associated with snack preparation and cleanup. Refer to the book to show children what to do if they forget to clean up after

continued on next page

eating. (Referring to the book throughout the various activities is an excellent means of developing the use of books as reference sources.)

Art Activity: The children create a collage depicting their chores either at home or at school. Use pictures from magazines, old cards, or calendars, or have children draw the pictures. Then have them label each picture.

Unit 3

Book: *Blue Sea* by Robert Kalan

Story Focus:

water	size comparisons
sea life	floating and sinking
fish	swimming
colors	chasing and escaping
net	getting stuck
food chain	environment

Writing Suggestions

Draw: how each fish got stuck.

yourself fishing.

where you think the little fish should hide.

what you like to do in water.

other things the big fish could eat.

where the little fish should go now.

your home (environment).

the kind of food you like to eat (food chain).

Extension Activities

Music: "Three Little Fishies" (Saxie Dowell, 1939)
"Row, Row, Row Your Boat"
"Baby Beluga" (Raffi, 1987)

continued on next page

Snacks: tuna sandwiches
sardines
goldfish crackers
clam chowder
blue gelatin with gummy worms or gummy fish
banana split boats filled with fruit or other healthy foods
celery boats filled with peanut butter, cream cheese, etc.

Other Activities:

Aquarium

Recreate the story in an aquarium. Have the children generate a list of needed items by reviewing the book. Problem-solve how to make the items and arrange them in the aquarium.

Water Table

Set up a water table. Provide objects that will sink and float, and allow children time to experiment with them. Assist the children in charting objects that sink versus objects that float. Children can also use objects to enact the story in the water.

Unit 4

Book: *The Birthday Party* by Ellyn L. Arwood*

Story Focus:

party (food, games)	emotions
age (years)	guests
friends	wishes
presents	invitations
giving and receiving	sequence of events

Writing Suggestions

Draw: a present you received for your birthday.

friends who came to your birthday party.

a game you would like to play at a party.

continued on next page

*Arwood, Ellen Lucas, Ed.D., CCC-SLP (1985). *APRICOT I.* Reprinted with permission of Apricot, Inc.; PO Box 18191; Portland, OR 97218.

your favorite part of a birthday party.

a place you went for a birthday party.

what will happen after the boy opens his presents.

what you think is in the package the boy is opening.

the kind of cake you would like for your next birthday.

thank-you notes for a gift.

Extension Activities

Music: "Happy Birthday"
"For He's a Jolly Good Fellow"
"If You're Happy and You Know It"
"London Bridge Is Falling Down"
"Ring Around the Rosie"

Snacks: homemade ice cream
cupcakes
punch
appetizers

Coffee-Can Ice Cream (8-10 Servings)

Make homemade ice cream in a can. You will need a three-pound and a one-pound coffee can, each with a lid.

2 cups cream	crushed ice
2 cups milk	rock salt
1 cup sugar	
1 tablespoon vanilla	
¼ teaspoon salt	

Fill the small coffee can with the cream, milk, sugar, vanilla, and salt. Stir the ingredients until the sugar is dissolved. Put the lid on the small can, and place it inside the big can. Pack crushed ice and rock salt around the small can. Put the lid on the big can. Make sure both lids fit tightly. Have the children roll the can back and forth until the ice cream is softly set (approximately 15-20 minutes).

continued on next page

Art Activities:

Invitations or Birthday Cards

Design invitations or make birthday cards. Talk with the children about the elements that characterize invitations or birthday cards before beginning the project.

Invitation

Name of honored guest
Date
Time
Place

Birthday Card

Poem or greeting
Signature

Be sure to have the children create envelopes for their invitations and cards.

Presents

To develop the idea of giving and receiving, have each child make a present for another child. For groups of children, draw names so everyone will give and receive a present.

Next have the children make wrapping paper for their gifts. Provide newsprint that the children can decorate with sponges or cut vegetables dipped in paints, ink stamps, stickers, markers, crayons, glitter, ribbon, etc. This activity may take several sessions to complete. The gifts could then be exchanged at a party.

Unit 5

Book: *The Three Little Pigs*

Story Focus:

sequence	danger
homes (parts)	guests
building	wishes
building materials	invitations
strong	tricky/clever
weak	animals
size	growing up
problem-solving	leaving home
mean	blowing
strength	helping
emotions (sad, scared, happy)	

Writing Suggestions

Draw: how the little pigs looked when they left home.

your house (apartment, mobile home, condo, etc.).

yourself building a house.

the wolf trying to get into one of the little pigs' houses.

what the pig's house looked like when the wolf blew it down.

a house the wolf would not be able to blow down.

other animals that are dangerous or mean.

how the third little pig tricked the wolf.

what the pigs did after they chased away the wolf.

Extension Activities

Music: "Who's Afraid of the Big Bad Wolf?"
"I Built My House" (tune: "The Farmer in the Dell")

continued on next page

I Built My House

I built my house of straw,
I built my house of straw,
And now it's time to sing and dance.
I built my house of straw.

I built my house of sticks.
I built my house of sticks.
And now it's time to sing and dance.
I built my house of sticks.

I built my house of brick,
I built my house of brick,
And don't have time to sing and dance.
I built my house of brick.

Snacks: pretzel-stick haystacks
gelatin bricks
pigs in a blanket
graham crackers to build a house

Gelatin Bricks

Prepare gelatin following the jiggler recipe on the box. Have the children cut the gelatin into rectangles to represent the bricks of the house. Talk about the physical similarities and differences between real bricks and the gelatin.

Art Activities:

Build a House

Invite the children to build a house. Supply an assortment of materials (craft sticks, blocks, twigs, drinking straws, packing peanuts, meat trays, milk cartons, etc.) for the project. Before building begins, ask the children to draw a picture of the house to use as a blueprint while they build their houses.

continued on next page

Paper-Bag Houses

Cut the corners off the top of a lunch bag to create a pointed roof. Have the children glue sticks on one bag, straw on another, and red paper bricks on the third. Put about one cup of sand inside the brick house bag, and staple it closed. Have the children huff and puff to try to blow down each of the three paper-bag houses.

Play Props and Scenery

Create the scenery for dramatic play. Brainstorm what objects or backdrops are needed for each scene.

Dramatic Play: Brainstorm ideas for costumes and scenery needed for a play about the story. Use art time to create the needed items. Dramatize the story by having the children role-play the different scenes of the story. Involve the audience by having the children boo and hiss when the wolf is bad.

Parents are an integral part of their children's development, so professionals who work with young children need to collaborate with parents. This chapter includes suggestions professionals may offer parents to help them facilitate their children's literacy development.

Keep in mind that parents may need varying levels of assistance to make these activities true literacy experiences.

Activities

Activity 1

Regularly read bedtime stories with the child. Choose stories from a variety of literary genres, including fairy tales, realistic stories, and poems. For a change of pace, use books of varying shapes and sizes.

Activity 2

Provide the child with a variety of materials and tools to allow experimentation with different modes of writing. Consider making available paper of various sizes, colors, and textures. Offer a choice of writing utensils, including crayons, pencils, markers, pens, felt pens, paints, or chalk. Allow the child to use a typewriter or a computer for writing activities.

Activity 3

Use a calendar to mark special events. Use pictures, stickers, writing, or a combination of symbols to mark events. Have the child read the calendar to identify activities for the day or special events that have been marked. Below is an example of a completed calendar form; a blank form is located on page 128.

Month __July__   Year __2000__

Sunday	Monday	Tuesday	Wednesday	Thursday	Friday	Saturday
						1 Go to grandma's
2 Picnic family reunion	3 swim lessons	4 Independence Day	5	6	7 We go home	8
9	10	11	12 riding	13	14	15
16	17 library	18	19	20	21	22
23	24	25	26	27 swimming lessons	28	29
30	31					

						Sunday
						Monday
						Tuesday
						Wednesday
						Thursday
						Friday
						Saturday

Month _____ Year _____

Activity 4

Use the form on page 130 to help the child create a weekly job schedule. Use pictures and words to represent the child's chores (see the example below). When it is chore time, help the child read the schedule to find the chore to be completed. Have the child mark off each job as it is finished.

Weekly Job Schedule

These are my jobs to do this week.

Sunday		Set the table.
Monday		Water the plants.
Tuesday		Put your dishes in the dishwasher.
Wednesday		Take out the trash.
Thursday		Feed the dog.
Friday		Put dirty clothes in the basket.
Saturday		Make cookies.

Weekly Job Schedule

These are my jobs to do this week.

Sunday	
Monday	
Tuesday	
Wednesday	
Thursday	
Friday	
Saturday	

Activity 5

Write notes to and with the child. Notes may be written with pictures, conventional writing, or a combination of the two. Put notes in the child's backpack to be read at day care or school.

Mrs. Chou,

I got a new

Kitten.

Activity 6

Help the child write a note to Mom or Dad. Leave the note on the parent's pillow to read before going to bed. (The child may leave a note anywhere the recipient would be sure to find it.)

Activity 7

Assist the child in writing or drawing thank-you notes, birthday cards, or get-well cards for friends or relatives. Provide old cards as examples of how to make a card, or use parts of old cards to construct a new card. Talk with the child about the message in the card before the child begins to write.

Activity 8

Have the child help write or draw a grocery list (see example below). Use the newspaper to find items on sale, or look through coupons for items on the list. While in the grocery store, read the list with the child as you look for the items listed.

Lists may be written for any kind of shopping.

Activity 9

Have the child plan a favorite meal once a week. Help the child write and/or draw the menu for the meal. Once the favorite meal is planned, use recipe cards and have the child help with the preparation. The child can help with all meals, not just the favorite one. Use pictures to write simple recipes, as in the sample below.

My Favorite Meal

macaroni and cheese

To cooked macaroni, add

Milk   1 cup = ▭

Butter   1 tablespoon = ▯

cheese   cheese packet

stir   and   eat.

Activity 10

Help the child make a "My Top 5" list of favorite songs. The child may also write the lyrics to the songs, draw pictures about the songs, or write new lyrics for old favorites. Sing these or other songs regularly with the child.

Activity 11

Set aside time to draw and/or write with the child. Topics for drawing and writing may be daily events, a trip to the park or zoo, a story that's been read, or any topic of interest. Then have the child read the story to a family member.

Activity 12

When planning a vacation, take the child to the library to find books or CDs about the destination. Access similar types of information via the Internet. Include the child in searching for the information. When all the information is collected, the child may draw or write about the places or things of interest. While on vacation, help the child write and send postcards to friends and relatives.

Activity 13

Play board or card games that require reading. Help the child create a family game that incorporates words or pictures of familiar items, such as names of favorite toys, family members, or animals.

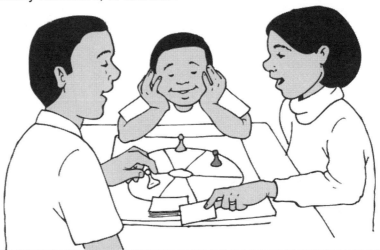

Activity 14

Help the child read cards and other correspondence received. While reading, take time to point out special features of the correspondence, such as the signature that indicates who sent the card.

Activity 15

Assist the child in writing letters or e-mails to friends and relatives. Ask the recipients to write back. Then help the child read the responses when they arrive.

The preceding activities describe a variety of ways parents can incorporate literacy experiences into everyday events in the home. The following Parent Literacy Inventory, pages 140-141, is another means for professionals to assist parents in examining the frequency and types of reading and writing experiences they provide children. It is not intended as an assessment tool, but rather as a means to heighten parental awareness of what they currently are doing and what additional literacy opportunities they can provide.

Parent Literacy Inventory

Reading

_____ I read with my child almost every day.

_____ I have a regular time to read with my child.

_____ I read the same book to my child several days in a row.

_____ I read the words in the book.

_____ I point to and label the pictures.

_____ I comment on and talk about the pictures.

_____ I point to the words as I read.

_____ I ask my child to point to pictures.

_____ I ask my child to label and comment on the pictures.

_____ I ask my child to tell me about the story.

_____ I ask my child to read the story.

_____ I ask my child to tell "why something happened" in the story.

_____ I ask my child to tell "what will happen next" in the story.

_____ I read magazines and newspapers with my child.

_____ I read signs and labels in the environment to my child.

_____ My child reads "special" recipes for making something to eat.

_____ My child sees me read books, magazines, or newspapers every day.

_____ I take my child to the library frequently.

_____ Other family members often read with my child.

_____ My child receives cards and/or letters in the mail.

_____ My child looks at catalogs, newspapers, and magazines.

Writing

_____ I write with my child almost every day.

_____ I have a regular time and place to write with my child.

_____ I write notes to my child.

_____ My child has a special place for his or her own writing supplies.

_____ My child helps make grocery lists.

_____ My child writes on a calendar.

_____ My child draws pictures for me and others.

_____ My child pretends to write stories about pictures.

_____ My child copies letters from books, magazines, or other print sources.

_____ My child plays with magnetic letters or blocks containing letters.

_____ I read stories from my child's pictures, pretend writing, and alphabet letters.

_____ I write dictated stories about my child's pictures.

_____ I write words and letters for my child to copy.

_____ My child makes cards for others (birthday, Valentine's Day, etc.).

_____ My child writes and sends cards and letters to others.

_____ My child draws and/or writes thank-you notes for gifts received.

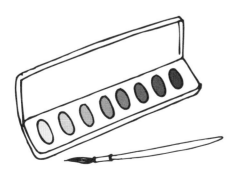
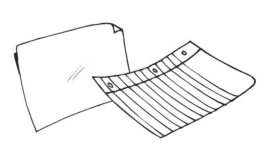

Children's Books

Ahlberg, J. & Ahlberg, A. (1981). *Peek-a-boo.* New York: Penguin Books.

Argueta, B. (1998). *Baby faces.* New York: Dutton Children's Books.

Aruego, J. & Dewey, A. (1989). *Five little ducks.* New York: Crown Publishers.

Berenstain, S. & Berenstain, J. (1983). *The Berenstain bears and the messy room.* New York: Random House.

Brett, J. (1996). *The mitten.* New York: Putnam Publishing Group.

Bridwell, N. (1972). *The Clifford series.* New York: Scholastic.

Brown, M. W. (1991). *Goodnight moon.* New York: HarperFestival.

Brown, M. W. (1995). *Big red barn.* New York: HarperFestival.

Carle, E. (1969). *The very hungry caterpillar.* New York: Philomel Books.

Carle, E. (1995). *The very busy spider.* New York: Philomel Books.

Carlson, N. L. (1990). *I like me.* New York: Penguin Putnam Books for Young Readers.

Christelow, E. (1989). *Five little monkeys.* New York: Clarion Books.

Cowley, J. (1990). *Hairy bear.* Bothell, WA: The Wright Group.

Cowley, J. (1990). *Mrs. Wishy-washy.* Bothell, WA: The Wright Group.

Elliott, R. (1996). *My cuddly toys.* Kuttawa, KY: McClanahan Book Co.

Fletcher, R. (1998). *Baby is hungry.* New York: Dutton Children's Books.

Galdone, P. (1970). *The three little pigs.* New York: Clarion Books.

Galdone, P. (1973). *The little red hen.* New York: Scholastic.

Galdone, P. (1973). *The three bears.* New York: Scholastic.

Ganker, G., Watson, D., Kromka, J., & Benjamin, A. (1997). *Goodnight baby Mickey.* New York: Golden Books.

Kalan, R. (1992). *Blue sea.* New York: William Morrow & Co.

Keats, E. J. (1976). *The snowy day.* New York: Penguin Putnam Books for Young Readers.

Martin, B. Jr. (1991). *Polar bear, polar bear, what do you hear?* New York: Henry Holt & Co.

Martin, B. Jr. (1996). *Brown bear, brown bear, what do you see?* New York: Henry Holt & Co.

Mayer, M. (1975). *Just for you.* Racine, WI: Western Publishing.

Mayer, M. (1983). *All by myself.* Racine, WI: Western Publishing.

Mayer, M. (1983). *Little Critter's this is my house.* Racine, WI: Western Publishing.

Mayer, M. (1983). *When I get bigger.* Racine, WI: Western Publishing.

Mayer, M. (1985). *I was so mad.* New York: Golden Books.

Mayer, M. (1985). *Just go to bed.* New York: Golden Books.

Mayer, M. (1987). *There's an alligator under my bed.* New York: E.P. Dutton.

Mayer, M. (1988). *I just forgot.* Racine, WI: Western Publishing.

Mayer, M. & Mayer, M. (1987-1992). *A boy, a dog, and a frog series.* New York: Dial Books for Young Readers.

Mosel, A. (1968). *Rikki tikki tembo.* New York: Scholastic.

Neitzel, S. (1989). *The jacket I wear in the snow.* New York: Greenwillow Press.

Noble, T. H. & Kellogg, K. (1992). *The day Jimmy's boa ate the wash.* New York: E.P. Dutton.

Numeroff, L. J. (1985). *If you give a mouse a cookie.* New York: Harper Collins Juvenile Books.

Pfloog, J. (1975). *Puppies are like that.* New York: Random House.

Quinlan, P. M. (1996). *Baby's feet.* North York, Ontario, Canada: Annick Press.

Sendak, M. (1962). *Chicken soup with rice.* New York: Harper Collins Children's Books.

Sendak, M. (1971). *Where the wild things are.* New York: Penguin.

Wade, L. (1998). *The Cheerios play book.* New York: Simon & Schuster.

Wellington, M. (1997). *Baby at home.* New York: Dutton Books.

Zeifert, H. (1995). *The three billy goats gruff.* New York: Tambourine Books.

Recommended Readings

Arwood, E. (1985). *Apricot I Kit (2nd ed.).* Portland, OR: Apricot.

Calkins, L. M. (1994). *The art of teaching writing (2nd ed.).* Portsmouth, NH: Heinemann.

Kemper, D., Nathan, R., & Sebranek, P. (1994). *Writers express: A handbook for young writers, thinkers, and learners.* Burlington, WI: Write Source Educational Publishing House.

Linder, T. W. (1999). *Read, play, and learn: Storybook activities for young children.* Baltimore: Paul H. Brookes Publishing.

Neuman, S. B., Copple, C., & Bredekamp, S. (2000). *Learning to read and write: Developmentally appropriate practices for young children.* Washington, DC: National Association for the Education of Young Children.

Norris, J. (1992). Learning to talk through literacy: Whole language for handi-capped preschoolers. In *Perspectives on whole language: Past, present, potential* (pp. 148-156). Columbia, MO: Instructional Materials Laboratory, University of Missouri.

Norris, J., & Hoffman, P. (1993). *Whole language intervention for school-age children.* San Diego: Singular Publishing.

Norris, J. A., & Hoffman, P. R. (1990). Language intervention within naturalistic environments. *Language, Speech, and Hearing Services in Schools, 21*, 72-84.

Norris, J. A., & Hoffman, P. R. (1995). *Storybook centered themes: An inclusive whole language approach.* Tucson, AZ: Communication Skill Builders.

Norris, J. A., & Hoffman, P. R. (1995) *Topical unit 1: Community and society curriculum.* Tucson, AZ: Communication Skill Builders.

Norris, J. A., & Hoffman, P. R. (1995) *Topical unit 2: Holidays and customs.* Tucson, AZ: Communication Skill Builders.

Norris, J. A., & Hoffman, P. R. (1995). *Topical unit 3: Me and my world.* Tucson, AZ: Communication Skill Builders.

Norris, J. A., & Hoffman, P. R. (1995) *Topical unit 4: Spring and the environment.* Tucson, AZ: Communication Skill Builders.

Olson, J. L. (1992). *Envisioning writing: Toward an integration of drawing and writing.* Portsmouth, NH: Heinemann.

Parker, R. P., & Davis, F. A. (Eds.). (1983). *Developing literacy: Young children's use of language.* Newark, DE: International Reading Association.

Pontecorvo, C., Orsolini, M., Burge, B., & Resnick, L. B. (Eds.). (1996). *Children's early text construction.* Mahwah, NJ: Lawrence Erlbaum.

Rothkopf, E. Z. (Ed.). (1986). *Review of research in education, 13.* Washington, DC: American Educational Research Association.

Snow, C. E., Burns, M. S., & Griffin, P. (Eds.). (1998). *Preventing reading difficulties in young children.* Washington, DC: National Academy Press.

Soderman, A. K., Gregory, K. M., & O'Neill, L. T. (1999). *Scaffolding emergent literacy: A child-centered approach for preschool through grade 5.* Needham Heights, MA: Allyn & Bacon.

Teale, W. H., & Sulzby, E. (Eds.). (1986). *Emergent literacy: Writing and reading.* Norwood, NJ: Ablex Publishing.

The Wright Group (1990). *The story box: Level 1 teacher guide.* Bothell, WA: The Wright Group.

References

Adams, M. J. (1990). *Beginning to read: Thinking and learning about print.* Cambridge, MA: MIT Press.

Altwerger, B., Diehl-Faxon, J., & Dockstader-Anderson, K. (1985). Read-aloud events as meaning construction. *Language Arts, 62,* 476-484.

Anderson-Yockel, J., & Haynes, W. O. (1994). Joint book-reading strategies in working-class African American and white mother-toddler dyads. *Journal of Speech and Hearing Research, 37,* 583-593.

Applebee, A. N. (1978). *A child's concept of story: Ages 2-17.* Chicago: University of Chicago Press.

Aram, D. M., & Hall, N. E. (1989). Longitudinal follow-up of children with preschool communication disorders: Treatment implications. *School Psychology Review, 18*(4), 487-501.

Arwood, E. L. (1985). *Apricot I.* Portland, OR: Apricot <http.//www.spiritone.com/~apricot>.

Bornstein, M., Toda, S., Azuma, H., Tamis-Lemonda, C., & Ogino, M. (1990). Mother and infant activity and interaction in Japan and the United States: II. A comparative microanalysis of naturalistic exchanges focused on the organization of infant attention. *International Journal of Behavioral Development, 13*(3), 289-308.

Bridwell, N. (1972). *Clifford the small red puppy.* New York: Scholastic.

Brinton, B., & Fujiki, M. (1993). Language, social skills, and socioemotional behavior. *Language, Speech, and Hearing Services in Schools, 24,* 194-198.

Bruner, J. (1967). On cognitive growth. In J. S. Bruner, R. R. Olver, P. M. Greenfield, J. R. Hornsby, H. J. Kenney, M. Maccoby, N. Modiano, F. A. Mosher, D. R. Olson, M. C. Potter, L. C. Reich, & A. M. Sonstroem (Eds.), *Studies in cognitive growth: A collaboration at the center for cognitive studies* (pp. 1-67). New York: John Wiley & Sons.

Chall, J. S., & Curtis, M. E., (1991). Responding to individual differences among language learners: Children at risk. In J. Flood, J. M. Jensen, D. Lapp, & J. R. Squire (Eds.), *Handbook of research on teaching the English language arts* (pp. 349-355). New York: Macmillan Publishing.

Clay, M. M. (1975). *What did I write?* Auckland, New Zealand: Heinemann.

Clay, M. M. (1979). *Reading: The patterning of complex behaviour (2nd ed.).* Auckland, New Zealand: Heinemann Educational.

Cowley, J. (1990). *Mrs. Wishy-washy.* Bothell, WA: The Wright Group.

Crowe, L. K. (1996). *Training parents to facilitate language through storybook reading.* Unpublished doctoral dissertation, Louisiana State University, Baton Rouge.

Crowe, L. K. (2000). Reading behaviors of mothers and their children with language impairment during repeated storybook reading. *Journal of Communication Disorders,36 (6)*, 503-524.

Crowe, L. K., Norris, J. A., & Hoffman, P. R. (2000). Facilitating storybook interactions between mothers and their preschoolers with language impairment. *Communication Disorders Quarterly, 21* (3), 131-146.

Damico, J. S., & Damico, S. K. (1993). Clinical forum: Language and social skills in the school-age population. Language and social skills from a diversity perspective: Considerations for the speech-language pathologist. *Language, Speech, and Hearing Services in Schools, 24,* 236-243.

Ferreiro, E. (1986). The interplay between information and assimilation in beginning literacy. In W. H. Teale & E. Sulzby (Eds.), *Emergent literacy: Writing and reading* (pp.15-49). Norwood, NJ: Ablex.

Gaitskell, C. D., Horowitz, A., & Day, M. (1982). *Children and their art.* New York: Harcourt Brace Jovanovich.

Gentry, J. R. (1982). An analysis of developmental spelling in GNYS AT WRK. *The Reading Teacher, 36,* 192-200.

Gertner, B. L., Rice, M. L., & Hadley, P. A. (1994). Influence of communicative competence on peer preferences in a preschool classroom. *Journal of Speech and Hearing Research, 37,* 913-923.

Halliday, M. A. K. (1978). *Language as a social semiotic: The social interpretation of language and meaning.* Baltimore, MD: University Park Press.

Harrison, C. (1999). Visual representation of the young gifted child. *Roeper Review, 21*(3), 189-194.

Hart, B., & Risley, T. R. (1999). *The social world of children learning to talk.* Baltimore: Paul H. Brookes Publishing.

Heath, S. B. (1983). *Ways with words: Language, life, and work in communities and classrooms.* Cambridge, England: Cambridge University Press.

Henderson, E., & Beers, J. W. (1980). *Developmental and cognitive aspects of learning to spell.* Newark, DE: International Reading Association.

Hess, R. D., & Holloway, S. (1984). Family and school as educational institutions. In R. D. Parke (Ed.), *Review of child development research, 7: The family* (pp. 179-222). Chicago: University of Chicago Press.

Juel, C., Griffith, P., & Gough, P. (1986). Acquisition of literacy: A longitudinal study of children in first and second grade. *Journal of Educational Psychology, 78,* 243-255.

Kaderavek, J. N., & Sulzby, E. (1997). *Oral narratives and emergent bookreadings of typically developing and language impaired children.* (ERIC Document Reproduction Service No. ED 420 850).

Kaderavek, J. N., & Sulzby, E. (1998). Parent-child joint book reading: An observational protocol for young children. *American Journal of Speech-Language Pathology, 7,* 33-47.

Kaderavek, J. N., & Sulzby, E. (2000). Issues in emergent literacy for children with language impairments. In L. R. Watson, E. R. Crais, & T. L. Layton (Eds.), *Handbook of early language impairment in children: Assessment and treatment* (pp. 199-244). Albany, NY: Delmar.

Kalan, R. (1992). *Blue sea.* New York: William Morrow & Co.

Kamhi, A. G., Catts, H. W., Maurer, D., Apel, K., & Gentry, B. F. (1988). Phonological and spatial processing abilities in language- and reading-impaired children. *Journal of Speech and Hearing Disorders, 53,* 316-327.

Kay-Raining Bird, E., & Vetter, D. K. (1994). Storytelling in Chippewa-Cree children. *Journal of Speech and Hearing Research, 37,* 1354-1368.

Klesius, J. P., & Griffith, P. L. (1996). Interactive storybook reading for at-risk learners. *The Reading Teacher, 49,* 552-560.

Langdon, H. W., & Cheng, L. L. (1992). *Hispanic children and adults with communication disorders: Assessment and intervention.* Gaithersburg, MD: Aspen.

Lapp, E. J. (1983.) *The blueberry bears.* Niles, IL: Albert Whitman.

Linderman, E. W., & Herberholz, D. W. (1972). *Developing artistic and perceptual awareness.* Dubuque, IA: William C. Brown.

Lonigan, C. J., Bloomfield, B. G., & Anthony, J. L. (1999). Relations among emergent literacy skills, behavior problems, and social competence in preschool children from low- and middle-income backgrounds. *Topics in Early Childhood Special Education, 19*(1), 40-53.

Lowenfeld, V., & Brittain, W. L. (1987). *Creative and mental growth (8th edition).* New York: Macmillan.

MacDonald, J. D. (1989). *Becoming partners with children: From play to conversation.* San Antonio, TX: Special Press.

Marvin, C. A., & Mirenda, P. (1993). Home literacy experiences of preschoolers enrolled in Head Start and special education programs. *Journal of Early Intervention, 17*(4), 351-367.

Marvin, C. A., & Wright, D. (1997). Literacy socialization in the homes of preschool children. *Language, Speech, and Hearing Services in Schools, 28,* 154-163.

Mason, J. A., & Allen, J. (1986). A review of emergent literacy with implications for research and practice in reading. In E. Z. Rothkopf (Ed.), *Review of research in education 13* (pp. 3-47). Washington, D.C.: American Educational Research Association.

Mattingly, I. (1972). Reading, the linguistic process, and linguistic awareness. In J. Kavanaugh & I. Mattingly (Eds.), *Language by ear and by eye* (pp. 133-149). Cambridge, MA: MIT Press.

Mayer, M. (1988). *I just forgot.* Racine, WI: Western Publishing.

Monroe, M. (1969). *Growing into reading.* New York: Greenwood Press.

Ninio, A., & Bruner, J. (1978). The achievement and antecedents of labeling. *Journal of Child Language, 5*(1), 1-15.

Norris, J. A. (1992). Learning to talk through literacy: Whole language for handicapped preschoolers. In *Perspectives on whole language: Past, present, potential* (pp. 148-156). Columbia, MO: Instructional Materials Laboratory, University of Missouri.

Norris, J. A. (1999a). *SDS-D: Functional observations of drawing in early childhood.* Unpublished Handout Presentation.

Norris, J. A. (1999b). *SDS-D: Functional observations of storybook reading in early childhood.* Unpublished Handout Presentation.

Norris, J. & Hoffman, P. (1993). *Whole language intervention for school-age children.* San Diego, CA: Singular.

Ochs, E. (1986). *Culture and language acquisition: Acquiring communicative competence in a western Samoan village.* New York: Cambridge University Press.

Raffi, & Pike, D. (1980). Baby beluga. [Recorded by Raffi & the Rise and Shine Band]. On *Raffi in concert with the Rise and Shine Band* [cassette]. Troubadour Records (1989).

Raffi, & Pike, D. (1987). Everything grows. [Recorded by Raffi & the Rise and Shine Band]. On *Raffi in concert with the Rise and Shine Band* [cassette]. Troubadour Records (1989).

Read, C. (1971). Preschool children's knowledge of English phonology. *Harvard Educational Review, 41,* 1-34.

Read, C. (1975). *Children's categorization of speech sounds in English: Research report No. 17.* Urbana, IL: National Council of Teachers of English.

Scarborough, H.S., & Dobrich, W. (1994). On the efficacy of reading to pre-schoolers. *Developmental Review, 14,* 245-302.

Shaywitz, S. E., & Shaywitz, B. A. (1993). Learning disabilities and attention deficits in the school setting. In L. J. Meltzer (Ed.), *Strategy assessment and instruction for students with learning disabilities: From theory to practice* (pp. 221-245). Austin, TX: PRO-ED.

Smith, S. S., & Dixon, R. G. (1995). Literacy concepts of low- and middle-class four-year-olds entering preschool. *Journal of Educational Research, 88,* 1309-1324.

Snow, C. E., Burns, S., & Griffin, P. (Eds.). (1998). *Preventing reading difficulties in young children.* Washington, DC: National Academy Press.

Snyder, L. S., & Downey, D. M. (1997). Developmental differences in the relation-ship between oral language deficits and reading. *Topics in Language Disorders, 17*(3), 27-40.

Sulzby, E. (1985). Children's emergent reading of favorite storybooks: A develop-mental study. *Reading Research Quarterly, 20*(4), 458-481.

Sulzby, E. (1989). Assessment of emergent writing and children's language while writing. In L. Morrow & J. Smith (Eds.), *The role of assessment in early literacy instruc-tion* (pp. 83-109). Englewood Cliffs, NJ: Prentice-Hall.

Sulzby, E., Barnhart, J., & Hieshima, J. A. (1989). Forms of writing and rereading from writing: A preliminary report. In J. M. Mason (Ed.), *Reading and writing connections* (pp. 31-63). Needham Heights, MA: Allyn and Bacon.

Teale, W. H., & Sulzby, E. (1986). *Emergent literacy: Writing and reading.* Norwood, NJ: Ablex.

Vygotsky, L. S. (1962). *Thought and language.* Cambridge, MA: MIT Press.

Vygotsky, L. S. (1978). *Mind and society: The development of higher psychological processes.* Cambridge: Harvard University Press.

Wells, C. G. (1985). Preschool literacy-related activities and success in school. In D. Olson, N. Torrance, & A. Hildyard (Eds.), *Literacy, language, and learning: The nature and consequences of reading and writing* (pp. 229-255). Cambridge, ENG: Cambridge University Press.

Westby, C. E. (1991). A scale for assessing children's pretend play. In C. Schaefer, K. Gitlin, & A. Sandgrun (Eds.), *Play diagnosis and assessment* (pp. 131-161). New York: Wiley & Sons.

Whitehurst, G. J., Arnold, D. S., Epstein, J. N., Angell, A. L., Smith, M., & Fischel, J. E. (1994). A picture book reading intervention in day care and home for children from low-income families. *Developmental Psychology, 30,* 679-689.

Whitehurst, G. J., Falco, F. L., Lonigan, C. J., Fischel, J. E., DeBaryshe, B. D., Valdez-Menchaca, M. C., & Caulfield, M. B. (1988). Accelerating language development through picture book reading. *Developmental Psychology, 24,* 552-559.

Wilson, M., & Wilson, B. (1982). *Teaching children to draw.* Englewood Cliffs, NJ: Prentice-Hall.

Yaden, D. B., Smolkin, L. B., & Conlon, A. (1989). Preschoolers' questions about pictures, print conventions, and story text during reading aloud at home. *Reading Research Quarterly, 24,* 188-214.

1-06-987654